ONCE YOU GO IN

Advance Praise for *Once You Go In*

"A deeply moving, searingly honest memoir of a young woman's emergence from a radical Pentecostal sect. Gelsinger tells her tale without animosity or self-pity, but with kindness and grace. We travel with her as she leaves behind the exacting God of her childhood, and begins to see glimpses of a Spirit that animates all that is around her. An inspiring book about claiming one's own freedom and finding the 'revival' within."

—Maggie Rowe, author of *Sin Bravely*

"With a keen eye for detail and a sharp skill for storytelling, Carly Gelsinger's *Once You Go In* is a must-read memoir for anyone searching for God in the aftermath of a shipwrecked faith experience. Gelsinger's wise and poignant writing reminds us that there is hope after a shipwreck, there is light after darkness and most of all, there is love even in the midst of pain."

—Elizabeth Esther, author of
Girl at the End of the World and *Spiritual Sobriety*

"Being a teenager is uncomfortable, desperate, and terrifying under the best circumstances; only much later can we look back and see the humor and magic of our most awkward years. The same is true of out-grown religion. We need space and time to integrate, recover, and laugh at the absurdity of it all. Carly Gelsinger does this with wisdom and candor: by exploring her past, she gives us permission to journey within our own."

—Reba Riley, author of *Post-Traumatic Church Syndrome:
One Woman's Desperate, Funny, and Healing Journey
to Explore 30 Religions by her 30th Birthday*

"I have read a lot of memoirs, but Carly Gelsinger's *Once You Go In* is one of the most profound pieces of storytelling I have ever encountered. It is the story of a young California girl who finds her way into a fundamentalist Pentecostal church and needs about a decade to find her way out again. The memoir unfolds slowly, as the naiveté of the young protagonist about where she is and what is happening to her dawns only very gradually. In the last third of the book we find ourselves cheering for Carly, hoping for her escape, for her rescue from those who were sure they knew where rescue could be found—in their own ignorant, exhausting, and, finally, very sad version of American Christianity. I cannot recommend this memoir highly enough, especially for those still trying to understand, or escape from, American fundamentalism."

—Dr. David Gushee, author of *Still Christian*
and president of the American Academy of Religion

"Carly Gelsinger's coming-of-age memoir is reminiscent of Judy Blume's *Are You There God, It's Me Margaret?*, only this time our heroine prays for transformation by the Holy Spirit! At times, her Pentecostal experience is so bizarre, you will be convinced you're reading fiction—but her adolescent journey is all too real. Carly exposes the truth about religious life, in that some things don't instantly change with the laying on of hands. Transformation takes time, patience, and sometimes, a little bit of rebellious faith."

—Jennifer Knapp, Grammy-nominated musician,
author of *Facing the Music: My Story*, and
founder of Inside Out Faith

"Vivid and engaging, this memoir shows, with honesty and intelligence, the appeal of Pentecostal religiosity to a sensitive and searching teenager... Gelsinger's excellent storytelling provides illuminating vignettes on her experience and how it was so often laced with doubt even as she sought certainty... A well-written, honest memoir that takes a multilayered view of revival."

—*Kirkus Review*

ONCE YOU GO IN

A Memoir of Radical Faith

Carly Gelsinger

Published 2018
Printed in the United States of America
ISBN: 978-1-63152-429-5 pbk
ISBN:. 978-1-63152-430-1 ebk
Library of Congress Control Number: 2018943326

For information, address:
She Writes Press
1569 Solano Ave #546
Berkeley, CA 94707

She Writes Press is a division of SparkPoint Studio, LLC.

In memory of Ilene Lampley,
whose unorthodox bravery lit a spark.

One

I used to get drunk on the Holy Spirit, but that was a long time ago. If Pastor Frank could see what I was getting drunk on now, he'd probably try to lay hands on me to pray the demons away. I thought of this as I ran my fingers over the surface of the long mahogany bar, taking in its nicks and bumps. I finished off my vodka and cranberry juice and laughed at something my friends said. To our left, strings of white lights sparkled over an exposed brick wall. A Katy Perry song blared over the bar's speakers, and a group of girls in furry boots and leggings were swaying and singing along behind us. On these Friday nights, deep into Boston's autumn, a tavern was the warmest and most festive place to be.

My friend Allie handed me a gin and tonic. I lapped up the top of the drink so it wouldn't spill. The taste instantly took me back to the pine needles I chewed as a child after I'd read of their high vitamin C content in a nature book.

"This tastes like a Douglas fir," I said.

"Have you not had gin before?" my friend Bea asked, squinting one eye at me.

"No, I have," I lied. I'm twenty-three years old. I should know what gin tastes like.

"Well cheers then," Bea said, pushing up her plastic-rimmed glasses. Bea was a gin-loving filmmaker, lesbian, and Red Sox fan who always had a camera strapped around her shoulders.

"To surviving another week," Allie said. She leaned across me to clink glasses with Bea. Allie was a sharp-witted blonde whom I bonded with on our first day of grad school over our penchant for Richard Nixon documentaries.

"To another weekend," I said, carefully clinking my glass up to both of theirs. When the gin hit my stomach, I felt warmth like a cozy fireplace spreading through my body. After spending my life trying to fit in, I had finally found people who were as nerdy as me, and all of a sudden, I didn't have to cloak myself to belong—mostly. There was one thing I did cloak, one Big Thing. My friends knew nothing of who I used to be—how I lived for mission trips and miracles, fasting and prophecy. I tried not to think about those times at all. My friends were at the bar to blow off academic steam. I came to forget. Sometimes the haze over those fiery Jesus days was so thick I could trick myself into believing they had never happened. But other times, I could feel the ashes buried deep in my soul, permeating everything.

I was an amateur drinker, really. Two years before, I'd had my first drink a month after my twenty-first birthday—a capful of Malibu Rum in a tumbler of pineapple juice, served by my "rebellious friend" from Christian college. I didn't even finish it because I was afraid of getting drunk. It didn't take me long after to learn that flooding my brain with booze was the easiest way to drown the memories.

The room was getting fuzzy, but I didn't stop. I ordered a basket of wings and a Long Island iced tea—another drink I'd heard of but never tried. Bea and Allie dug into the chicken, dipping the wings in ranch and buffalo sauces, while I gulped down my drink.

You were going to change the world, a voice popped into my head.

I leaned forward on my barstool and stared at my empty glass, where the reflection of tiny white lights spun in figure eights. I closed my eyes and rested my cheek on the cold bar.

But look at you now.

In the swirling darkness, Bea and Allie's faces faded, and a silver-haired man appeared, pacing at a pulpit and yelling. A woman sat behind him at a piano, her fingers cascading up and down the keys in a fluid motion. I heard a deep voice over the phone. *God has incredible plans for you.* I smelled mildewed carpet; my face pressed down on it. *Yes, Lord. Yes, Jesus. Yes, Lord.* Hot tears ran down my face.

"I'm backslidden," I blurted, without lifting my head from the bar. My armpits were damp with sweat.

"You're back-what?" Bea asked. "Carly, are you crying?"

"I used to be chosen. Consecrated. On fire," I said, pulling up my head and putting my mouth around the straw to suck up the melted ice. "But look where I am now."

"Well, I am glad you're here," Allie said, tipsy and generous. "Let's put some quarters in the jukebox. This bar could use a little Bruce Springsteen."

"I have to confess something, you guys," I continued. "I still like Jesus. Does that make me a crazy freak?"

"No, it doesn't make you a crazy freak," Bea said, then flagged the bartender to bring me a glass of ice water and then held it up to my mouth. "Drink this, hun."

"She okay?" the bartender asked.

"I think so," Allie said.

I took a long sip of water, and my stomach lurched.

"Let's get more Long Islands," I said, slurring my words.

"Drink the water first," Allie said. "Then we'll get more."

"And eat something. Here," Bea said, shoving a chicken wing

under my nose. I bit off a piece of meat and chewed it. My mouth felt rubbery.

"They were wrong. They were so wrong about everything," I said.

"Who is *they*, hun?" Bea asked.

"All of them. All of them," I said.

I fought back my gag reflex and drank some more water.

"Can't I have my Jesus and still believe you should be able to get married if you want to?" I asked Bea. "Because they say I can't."

Before I could get an answer, I dropped my tumbler, rupturing liquid with hundreds of glass shards all over the concrete floor. In a feeble attempt to clean up the mess, I grabbed a flimsy napkin and bent over. I lost my balance and hit the ground on my back. As I flailed around trying to stand, my stomach knotted up. A vile eruption of gin and rum and vodka and fried chicken flew from my throat, pieces of it landing on my sweater, Bea's shoes, and the barstool's legs.

"Oh, shit," Allie said. "Are you okay?"

"No more of them," I said, flat on my back and soaking in a puddle of brown vomit, a pile of broken glass next to me. "I can't do it. No more of them. Just Jesus. They can't take Jesus away from me."

"Get her out of here," the bartender yelled, as a bouncer came through with a giant push mop. The bouncer bent over and got in my face.

"Just Jesus," I said again.

"Okay, Jesus Girl, if you don't get the hell out of here in the next ten seconds, we'll call the cops," he said. He turned to Bea and Allie. "Get her gone. Now." My friends pulled me up, pushed my arms through the gray pea coat I had draped over my barstool, and each took a side of my limp body, carrying me out of the tavern and into the freezing New England night.

—

I gave my heart to Jesus at a Baptist Vacation Bible School when I was seven years old. In exchange, I was given a stuffed bunny, hand-stitched by one of the elderly church ladies. It was made with quilter's fabric, white with little green shamrocks. I put the bunny on a shelf overlooking my twin bed, where it watched me with its button eyes, making sure I was good day and night. Some would say this is when I found God, but I know otherwise.

I grew up in Pine Canyon, a northern California town tucked in the crevasses of the Sierra Nevada Mountains. By the time I was born in the 1980s, Pine Canyon had a population of about six hundred, its apex reached more than a hundred years before. Its bustling railroad-and-gold days long forgotten, Pine Canyon had tapered to families partial to a quiet mountain life. And quiet it was. Surrounded by red dirt, ponderosa pines, and two wild rushing rivers, Pine Canyon boasted more saloons than stoplights (four to none). Downtown was one block of brick-façade buildings, an Amtrak stop, an old movie theater, restaurants that could never stay open, and an antique-red caboose permanently parked outside the bank. A visit to town meant running into any number of people we knew, such as Wayne the Honest Mechanic, or Craig the Crooked Mechanic, or Bud the Honest-but-Alcoholic Mechanic. Besides mechanics, we might see Bill the Gold Miner and George the Greek talking outside the Railhead Saloon, or Dick the Cal-Trans Worker renting a movie from Pick-A-Flick Video, or Corinne the Artist, working on a chalk mural on the sidewalk outside the caboose. On more rare occasions, we could see Ice-Pick Ron, who had served time in prison for stabbing someone with—what else?—an ice pick. Or Peacock Bill, or Myrtle the Librarian, who was cranky because she had shingles, or Arnold and Ardith the Antiques Collectors and owners of the Mexican Villa where Mom had waited tables when she was pregnant with me. I belonged to these people before I could talk. To them, I was Tom the Painter's Daughter, a title I was proud of.

In the darkness of winter mornings, Dad would stoke the fire in our wood-burning stove before he left for work. I would wake to the *shree-shree-shree* of an old newspaper being torn into strips and the low roar of the fire, and I would burrow deeper under my covers, the ashy smell of the stove and its slow, creeping warmth lulling me in for more dreaming. As I slept, Dad pulled on his white carpenter pants every day, stained with whatever color he'd been rolling or spraying that week, and started his old blue Dodge van with the round headlights that I thought looked like stupefied eyes.

I would wake up a few hours later, and set about my day of exploring my parents' twelve forested acres and the nearby pond where I swung from ropes into mucky water and hunted for frogs with five legs. Often my younger brother, Paul, and I did these things instead of doing our schoolwork, and our teacher—Mom—allowed it because she believed childhoods should be long and free. Often, when I mention my homeschooling background, people think I come from one of those big families in matching jumpers who aren't taught science. We were different, I am quick to explain. We were the kind of homeschoolers who took a five-week trip to Baja California during the school year in an old RV. We studied Mexican history by visiting Oaxaca Indian villages and Spanish missions; we studied biology by snorkeling in the Sea of Cortez at low tide.

But the majority of my childhood memories are at home. We lived six miles northeast of town in a trailer—or something of a 1970s modular home—one that existed on the property when Mom bought it before she had children. Anytime my parents had a few extra dollars, it went into renovating the tin-roofed barn behind the trailer that they planned to someday turn into our rustic dream home. We called it the Barn, as in, "When we move to the Barn, we'll have room for a piano." In the meantime, they made the trailer homey with a wraparound deck covered with potted flowers and a porch swing that looked out to the canyon. I couldn't tell the difference between our house and our friends' houses until I was about ten years old and I realized most other families' front doors weren't made of aluminum. When I pointed this out to Mom, she said that the inside part of our house isn't much, but the outside part is vast with rivers and trees and meadows, and what matters more?

We spent most of our days in the outside part of our house, barefooted on the banks of the American River. I would be reading a torn copy of *Anne of Green Gables*. Dad would be ten yards upstream, panning for gold, while my brother waved a piece of driftwood in the air in an imaginary sword fight. Sometimes we would fish, and I always felt something profound, perhaps spiritual, in the tension of my rod when I hooked something—a rainbow trout, or more often, a clump of ragweed. I would eat the lunch Mom packed me that morning, and use the napkin she wrote a love note on as a bookmark. I'm not sure anyone can wipe their face with a handwritten note from their mother.

Most Sunday mornings were spent on a bench with Dad in downtown Pine Canyon. This ritual began when I was so small Dad had to lift me to drop the coins in the newspaper dispenser for his weekly paper. When Paul was old enough to see what he was missing, he wanted to come too. I reluctantly shared Dad on these mornings.

Dad always got a Dr. Pepper, and Paul and I always got purple Squeezits, a sugary "juice" in a squeezable plastic bottle. I never was allowed Squeezits on Mom's watch, so these were special times. Dad would utter this high-pitched whistle lacking any melody, like the sound you make when you blow into a shell, as he flipped through the paper always in this order: front page, sports, comics. Toss the lifestyle section. We would wait for the train, always signaled by one long horn. Paul wore his conductor's hat and jumped up and down at its arrival. I would stare into the sleeper cars of the Amtrak and hope someday I could be as fancy as the people sleeping on the train.

Until somebody told me years later, I didn't know I was supposed to be in church on Sundays. I didn't know that people were driving by us, dressed in their Sunday best, probably thinking about how we kids needed saving. I didn't know that Sunday mornings were meant for anything other than watching the trains go by with Dad.

I decided when I was very young that my father was my hero, so even the night Mom screamed and dug her fingers into a Christmas casserole and flung pieces at him when he came home drunk again, I couldn't muster anger for him. I hid in my bedroom as the fight went on—*scream, splat, scream, splat*—reading the yellowed pages of my book by dim lamp. Dad later came to kiss me goodnight, pieces of egg and canned Ortega chilies still stuck to his red flannel shirt. I could smell beer on his breath as his prickly cheek brushed my forehead. I didn't kiss him back because I had to teach him a lesson, not because I didn't want to.

When Dad moved out a few months later, I realized my world was as fragile as those dragonflies with missing wings we saw at the pond. I tried to be strong for Paul, who understood even less than I did. One night, we watched *Star Wars*. Paul wept the entire movie and begged Mom to let us visit Dad. We piled in the car and drove to the river cabin Dad lived at, but when we got there, Mom said Dad was too drunk to be near us. She took us to get personal pizzas instead.

The day Dad came back, I was petting our Labrador on the deck. He crept up behind me with a take-and-bake pizza in his arms.

"I'm sorry," he said. Dad wasn't one of those men who never cried, but usually he tried to wipe his tears. This time, he let them fall from his face and down the cracks of the wooden deck he built by hand. "I'm going to change," he said, tears splatting on the wood. "I'm home"—*splat*. "I'm going to be a Dad again"—*splat*. I believed him, because that's what six-year-old girls do for their fathers. Lucky for me, he told the truth.

A few years later on that same deck, which had been painted over twice and had many boards replaced, the four of us sat around a weathered table in a game of Rummy. The Beatles' *Magical Mystery Tour* played in the background on my brother's gray Sony compact disc player he got for Christmas that year, which weighed as much as a watermelon.

The Beatles were in the background of everything we did, playing on that stereo. Paul and I were on a mission to collect every song the Beatles ever made. We took turns using our allowance for the cause.

We sang "All You Need is Love" as the sun set behind the wall of pine trees next to us, and something filled our voices, something found in John Lennon's ripe-peach voice, so soft yet prickly, and the most honest voice I'd ever heard. We sang with weight behind our smiles. My heart bubbled over with the sense that love filled our lungs, and that love was bigger than the canyon surrounding us.

Perhaps for these reasons, I had an inexplicable draw to be near God from a young age. Maybe that's what led me to Pine Canyon Assemblies of God Church, or maybe it was something less spiritual, less fateful. Maybe it was simply because I biked by it on a day I wished I had more friends.

Occasionally, if Mom had an appointment in the big city, she would drop Paul and me off in Pine Canyon with our bikes and packed lunches. We would ride to the library and lean our bikes outside the entrance without locking them, and spend a couple hours reading on scratchy mustard yellow armchairs. The library was usually empty, except for the one guy who came in every morning to do the crossword puzzle. Most kids our age were in school.

When we tired of sitting, we would check out a few books, slip them into our backpacks, and ride down Main Street. We liked to sneak into the ice cream shop for scoops of Rocky Road and a game or two of Pac-Man. Next door, Bud the Mechanic would be leaning against a beam, smoking outside the Railhead Saloon. He would say something about how Tom the Painter's kids are getting so big he could hardly recognize us. He might try to tell us a town legend or two, about the ghost that lives in the abandoned hotel, or the real reason no restaurant can make it in the old bank building.

We would laugh Bud off and keep riding around town until Mom picked us up.

On one particular day, we find ourselves on Grove Street, a part of town we've never explored before. We maneuver our bikes around deep potholes and portions of upturned sidewalk. At the end of the street, we happen upon a little gray church with cracked stucco walls and a wooden cross nailed above the entrance. A vinyl banner hanging from the roof says VOICE IN THE DESERT YOUTH, 7 P.M. THURSDAYS.

Youth. The word makes me picture slumber parties and pepperoni pizza and group photos and matching T-shirts. The Baptist church I've been going to off and on for years doesn't have *Youth*. They have babies and old people, and Vacation Bible School, which is for little kids. I wonder what it would be like to have a group, a place to belong.

I have heard about this church before. The legend around town is that when the Spirit pays a visit to the little church on Grove Street—which it does reliably every Sunday morning and evening, Wednesday, and Thursday—the racket is greater than that of the freight trains screeching through the heart of town. They say the windows are frosted glass so nobody on the outside can see what goes on inside. They say once you go in, you never come out. Many Pine Canyon legends are tall tales, told by people who have had a few too many Coors Lights at the saloon.

But sometimes the legends are true.

Two

I have only been attending Pine Canyon Assemblies of God for a few months when I find myself sweating under the morning sun, standing on the torn-up concrete in the church parking lot, listening to Pastor Frank's threats and wondering when exactly we will leave for summer camp. We were supposed to leave an hour ago.

"I will *personally* yank you out," says Pastor Frank Rowan, a gray-haired man, tall and broad-shouldered with a jiggly belly that hovers over strong legs.

Pastor Frank is only like this when he preaches, I remind myself. This isn't really him. Just ten minutes before, he was all hugs and grins as he hopped out of his dented blue Volkswagen Bus to send us off to camp with a blessing.

"If I get wind that there is even a hint of the Spirit of Disobedience or the Spirit of Rebellion, you are in for it. Do you understand?" His sagging, iguana jowls shake. I haven't seen him this upset before, and it makes me nervous.

Let's say I ran into Pastor Frank on the street, like he was a mailman or a dog walker or something other than a pastor. I'd say he was a jolly guy, a down-to-earth man with a kind heart, and I wouldn't have been wrong. Unless Pastor Frank is praying, or talking about the Bible or sin, he *is* jolly, down-to-earth, and kind. But when he gets worked up like this, he frightens me. Others say it is the Fire of God burning through him, but I am not sure what they mean by that. The best thing I can think to do when Pastor Frank acts like this is to tell myself it will blow over soon. It always does, eventually.

"Your leaders are the people God gave you to lead you to him," Pastor Frank says. His hands are flying around his face in fists. "Do not take that lightly."

I'm thirteen and the newest member of the "Missionettes," Pine Canyon Assemblies of God's version of the Girl Scouts, only instead of selling cookies and working for badges, we memorize Scripture. Today I join six other junior high girls for my first-ever Christian summer camp.

Jessa Rowan—Pastor Frank's middle daughter, and one of our camp leaders—locks her giant blue eyes with me. I nod, acknowledging the gravitas of the moment. Jessa is beautiful to me; under her pale skin and frizzy brown hair, something powerful glows. Pastor Frank says it is the Holy Spirit shining through her. Jessa is hailed as the example for all of us adolescent girls in Missionettes. At twenty years old, she lives at home and is courting Jacob, an athletic, dark-haired, strong Christian from youth group who plays guitar at worship nights, which is the most romantic thing I can imagine. We all want Jessa's love story. I notice our other leader, nineteen-year-old Candace, is staring down at the ground, looking more somber than usual. I am pretty sure Candace has the Holy Spirit too, but not to Jessa's caliber.

"Can you commit to honoring your leaders in word and deed this week?" Pastor Frank says.

"Yes," all six of us mumble. We grip each other's hands and ask God to help us be good. Pastor Frank only wants to make sure we have a great time, and he knows that can't happen if we don't obey our leaders. I keep telling myself this.

I'm a good girl. I've never smoked or drunk or even kissed a boy, but I still haven't figured out this group and their rules. Sometimes I wonder if my personality is naturally sort of against their rules. I can be loud and unladylike and I speak my mind. Because of this, my best friend Jane's mom, Ilene, has called me her "Wild Child" since I was little. Just a week ago, she had to drag me out of a Ross Dress for Less because I was dancing around the swimsuit section belting out Broadway tunes like a derelict Vegas entertainer. Jane, a popular volleyball player in public school, got very mad because a boy she liked from class was in the store and saw the whole scene. Ilene couldn't stop laughing, even as she escorted me out of the store. I knew my behavior was unsuitable for a department store, but I couldn't seem to stop. Sometimes I snap like that. I hope it doesn't happen this week; I have a feeling Candace or Jessa wouldn't laugh if they saw Wild Child. I will have to be extra careful. The less I say, the better.

We say "Amen," and pile into the church minivan with rusty hubcaps and a veneer stripe down the sides. Pastor Frank smiles and waves us off.

"Be blessed, you women of God," he says. He appears to be back to his happy self.

I settle back in my seat, adjusting the soft pink eyelet handkerchief on my head. As soon as we pull away, the sun through the van window begins to reflect on my blonde leg hair, making it shine an iridescent gold.

Oh God, please no.

I am the only girl in this group—even including Dahlia, the other homeschooled one who is a year younger than me—who doesn't shave her legs yet. I know because the girls talk about shaving their legs all the time, a topic worthy of coming back to again and again. They swap funny stories of nicking themselves, or embarrassing tales of forgetting to shave the coarse hair that grows around the ankles. They talk about their favorite brands of razors and fruit scented shave gels.

Heather is the one who brings up shaving her legs the most. She joined the church six months before me after being delivered from Wicca. At least that's what she told me when we first met. The church took her under their wing and in just a few months, she grew to be majorly on fire for the Lord. She announces this regularly. Heather often shows up to Missionettes with freshly shaved legs and demands that the other girls run their hands up and down her calves and compliment her on their smoothness and sheen. She never asks me to do this because we are not friends. Actually, I don't have any friends in this group yet.

As long as I'm not in direct light, my leg hair is hardly noticeable. But here, with the California July sun dancing on my lower body as we weave through traffic on the interstate, I can feel the stares of the public-schooled girls on me. I can't let this be the reason I don't make friends this week; I pull a sweatshirt out of my backpack and cover up my legs, even though I'm roasting in this van without air conditioning.

I snap out of my thoughts to hear Heather and the other girls laughing and singing a song that has been all over the radio the last few months. I don't know the singer (I pretty much only know Beatles and Broadway music), but I recognize it from trips to the grocery store and the dentist.

They sing, in a gravelly voice, kind of like the actual singer only not as good.

I am giggling and bobbing my head, hoping I look cool, hoping it will help me belong. When they get to the chorus, I join in, throwing out the only lyric of the song I know. Then they go back to the verses and I'm moving my mouth around silently, pretending I know the rest of the words.

From my position in the middle seat, I see Candace, in the passenger's seat, and Jessa, in the driver's seat, swap a look that involves raised eyebrows and pursed lips—not a good face for grown-ups to make.

Candace clears her throat.

"Let's not sing that song," she says, eyeing us from the rearview mirror.

"Why?" Heather asks. I'm glad Heather asked because I want to know too.

"Because it is secular," Candace says. "It does not honor God."

"Oh, okay," Heather says, unfazed. She starts leading the group in a song I have never heard before, not even in a grocery store.

"Yes, 'Jesus Freak'—that's a more appropriate song," Candace says, and nods approvingly.

As the girls get really into the chorus, singing loud and laughing with each other, my mind is spinning from what just happened. What is wrong with the song we were singing? What does *secular* mean? Why didn't Candace explain *why* the song was bad? Maybe because it's a song about a woman who tries to leave and "chokes." That must be it. Choking when trying to break up with someone isn't a very good thing I guess. Maybe "secular" had something to do with women in abusive relationships. Or maybe secular means things that don't talk about Jesus. That could very well be the case because this "Jesus Freak" song sure seems to talk a lot about Jesus. Am I supposed to mention Jesus every few minutes so I don't turn secular too?

I need to make sure I don't get in trouble again, but I don't know how because I don't know what I did wrong. I wonder how all the other girls were able to accept these kinds of lectures and stay so giddy. They are laughing like nothing happened. Maybe they understand things I do not. I'm just the furry-legged one who doesn't know the rules.

I want answers, but I am afraid to question Candace and Jessa. It seems like I should know this already, and Pastor Frank's warning is fresh in my mind. *Your leaders are the people God gave you to lead you to him.* I make a mental note to look up "secular" in the dictionary when I get home and to make sure to never do it around these people again.

I long to make friends, but at the same time, I am also suspicious of joining the crowd, and while Mom tells me this is a strength, it doesn't score me any cool points. I learned this the hard way a few years ago, when all my friends saw *Titanic* in the theater a dozen times, and I stayed home to make fun of all the conformists waiting in line to watch a boat sink. But alone in my bed, I'd secretly sing "My Heart Will Go On" and cry, just like everyone else. I thought it was the most beautiful song I'd ever heard.

I'm thinking of this as I find myself the only girl left in the pews as the Camp Lady, bleached hair rock-solid and sparkly gold jewelry glinting under the lights, cries out, "This is where you meet God!" More than two hundred girls are funneling down to the altar while I stay in my seat. "If you thirst for more of God, don't hesitate!" But I am hesitating, a wave of guilt running through me, that guilt being what they call "the Holy Spirit's nudge." Even Krissy and Amanda, two girls from Pine Canyon who come from atheist homes, are joining in.

But I don't move.

"Don't let Satan hold you back!"

I resolve to not show my tears to the hyper Camp Lady. Instead, I sit in my pew and get mentally prepared for the Crazy Slipper Contest that is scheduled after this, and which I am sure to win. The pianist slams the same four chords over and over, singing, "More of you, Jesus! More of you, God," and the girls wail along at the altar, all wanting more of God. The Camp Lady is pacing the stage with her hands raised in the air. I am pretty sure I am content with the amount of God in my life. I'm not even sure how someone can have more or less of God—like more or less ranch dressing on a salad? Isn't God already everywhere? But the other girls want more, and they are sobbing at the altar to get it.

"If you want to see Jesus tonight, let go of your inhibitions. Surrender! Open yourself up! Cry out to him, say 'Jesus, use me, use me, I am your vessel. Use me, Lord Jesus. Yes, Lord.' Shout it with me . . . Yes, Lord!" the Camp Lady says.

A funny feeling rises in my tummy, kind of like nervousness, but worse. The mood in the room seems to be escalating. I've seen altar calls before but nothing like this. Usually, for altar calls at the Baptist church, the preacher says a short prayer and then service ends and we get to go eat egg salad sandwiches. This is different—like the altar call itself is building to something else, something big. What that might be, I don't know, and I'm not sure I want to know. My stomach lurches again. I focus on a wooden beam on the ceiling of the creaky old chapel.

"Yes Lord! Yes Lord! Yes Lord!" the crowd chants.

So this is what church camp is like? Lots of people crying and singing together for a long time? My heartbeat picks up. I get the sense that nobody is in control of the room, that at any moment, something truly terrible could happen and nobody would stop it.

Desperate for a distraction, I pull out my notebook and begin doodling a picture of a cow.

Focus on the cow, I tell myself as one girl fills the room with obscene panting and barking noises.

"Yes Lord," the Camp Lady sings. Nobody tells the girl making the barking noises to stop, so she keeps going. "Do a mighty work in us tonight. Rain on us, Holy Spirit." The piano music raises a half step and gets louder.

The girls from my group are shaking and hugging each other and swaying back and forth, and Candace and Jessa have their hands on the tops of the girls' heads and are swaying to the music. Jessa glances in my direction and raises her eyebrows, and I can't tell if her face is of pity or disapproval, or both. I feel like I might be in trouble again.

Blood starts rushing to my hands. I can hear my heart pounding from my fingertips. *The Holy Spirit is terrifying,* I think. I draw a surfboard under my cow's hoofs.

"Ask the Lord to break you tonight," says the Camp Lady.

"Yes Lord, break me, break me, Holy Spirit, Jesus." The masses split off into spontaneous songs and prayers, each girl competing to be heard over the others.

I sketch a speech bubble for my surfer cow. "Cowabunga!" it says. I smile to myself, pleased with my pun.

One frizzy-haired girl with lots of acne seems to really be meeting the Spirit, whatever that means. She is praying and shaking fast, and then *bam*, like lightning, she falls to the floor in a fit of convulsions. These robotic groans are spewing from her mouth, and instead of helping her up, people are clapping for her.

"Rababa-rababobo, Oh shanana-rababo!" she says, her eyes rolling to the back of her head.

"The Holy Spirit has come mightily inside one of us," the Camp Lady screams. "May it spread like fire. Like fire! Like fire!"

"Like fire, like fire," the girls echo between sobs.

I can't concentrate on my stupid cow drawing anymore. The room is falling apart around me and people are screaming and talking in gibberish and it's all supposed to be from God. I try to breathe slowly but I can't stop gasping for air. I feel dizzy. I pray to God that he would make his Holy Spirit go away, but I worry God is too busy causing the frenzy fifteen feet away to hear my prayers. I'm shaking. I think about calling Mom to come get me, but that would be too embarrassing. Teenagers don't call their moms to pick them up.

I pull out my camp schedule from the back pocket of my overalls. The Crazy Slipper Contest is supposed to start in twenty minutes. I love the thrill of winning a contest, so in the weeks before camp, I prepared for this one by carefully decorating my cow slippers with slaughterhouse protest signs I constructed with foam letters, poster board, and Popsicle sticks.

Just as the room quiets down and I think it must finally be time to head over to the cafeteria where the slipper contest is supposed to be held, one girl screams over everyone else "Holy Spirit, boyokaveeeeechee!" and the Camp Lady says "Hallelujah!" and everyone starts praying and crying again, even louder than before.

Jessa and Candace and several other camp counselors are circled around Dahlia, the other homeschooled girl, who is also my roommate for the week. Tears and snot are running into her mouth, and they do not hand her a tissue. The counselors push her back and forth, each one catching her and then launching her into the arms of another. She sways deeper with each push, until the woman behind her lets her fall to the ground. Dahlia fans herself and thrashes her legs on the floor. Her shirt has crept up her waist to reveal a strip of white skin above her jeans. I watch one of the counselors reach into a box and pull out a thin blue blanket and gently cover Dahlia's midriff. The counselors nod to each other and circle another girl at the packed altar.

Push, sway, push, sway. Fall. Cover. Repeat.

I feel like I'm choking.

Please God, I beg. *Make it stop.*

At midnight, we finally walk back to our rooms, the girls satiated and our leaders proud.

"That was a thousand times better than any Crazy Slipper Contest," Jessa says, and the girls let out a laugh and agree.

"I don't know how I am going to explain this to my parents. It was so incredible. Jesus is amazing," Krissy says.

"Tell them about the power you saw tonight. Your heart is now filled with the Holy Spirit, and you are a completely new person. Your parents will start to be jealous for what you have in your heart," Jessa says, putting her arm around Krissy.

As for my heart, it is just starting to beat normally again.

I pick up on the rhythms of Pentecostal camp pretty fast. The morning church services present fun and lighthearted topics, such as how to dress cute without causing men to stumble. The afternoon services are a tad more serious—usually these are concerned with discussions about why dating is a slippery slope that can lead to backsliding, especially dating an unbeliever. Since I don't know any boys interested in dating me, Christian or not, that one seems easy.

But it is the evening services I fear. The messages are always on the power of the Holy Spirit, and the altar calls go late into the night. I still haven't gone forward at one of them. I am getting the feeling the other girls, and maybe even the leaders, are talking about Carly the Unspiritual One. They give me these looks after their altar calls, like I'm really missing out on something. Maybe I am.

On the second-to-last day of camp, Dahlia and I sit in the sand eating chocolate-dipped ice cream cones at the Santa Cruz Beach Boardwalk, talking about the Holy Spirit. We've broken off from the other girls, with orders to meet by the pirate ship ride at 4 p.m. It's been a whirlwind week with so many prayer meetings and altar calls—not at all what I expected camp to be like. We hadn't played any camp games or had s'mores or done any of the things I thought happened at normal camps. But we did get to go to the Boardwalk today, and I'm eating ice cream, so I guess I can't complain.

Dahlia Platt grew up in the church; her dad is a deacon and her mom is a striking woman with jet-black hair who shows up to every church event with a homemade meal and hugs for everyone. Dahlia has dark curly hair and pale skin, like a vintage movie star. Still, Dahlia is an outsider in Missionettes, a bit like me. We dig our toes in the sand and talk about the other girls in the group, and I get the feeling she likes me more than them. Out of everyone, I like her the most too. I'm thrilled to make a friend.

"You're not used to the Holy Spirit coming down, are you?" she asks.

"No, but I'm all for learning more about God and all that stuff," I say, licking a dribble of mint chip ice cream from my wrist.

"Yeah, I guess it's scary at first, but you get used to it, and pretty soon you crave it all the time," she says.

"It actually *really* scared me last night," I say. Dahlia doesn't respond, but she doesn't seem offended either. She almost seems like she regrets not having an answer. We watch a group of giggling girls our age in bikini tops and cutoff jeans walk by.

"Heather totally likes Mark, doesn't she?" she finally says. I feel relieved to venture back into the safer place of discussing other people's problems instead of our own.

"Yeah, she won't shut about him this whole trip. Seriously, everything is Mark, Mark, Mark," I say.

Dahlia convinces me to try the Hammerhead, a ride I've seen at county fairs but never dared to go on before. The ride straps people in metal crates and lurches forward and backward in a loop before suspending riders upside down at its highest point. The attendant is buckling us in these metal cages, and I feel that same jolt in my stomach I feel at the altar calls. *Just breathe.* The ride starts to move, slowly at first but gaining speed, faster, faster, then we are hurdled in the air, upside down and I feel like I'm being tortured and I want to be anywhere but where I am.

"Just relax," Dahlia says, above the creaks of the ride and the screams of its passengers.

I try to focus on breathing regularly, even as my whole body clinches up.

"Get me off, get me off! God, please make it stop," I sob, but the ride keeps going.

After two excruciating minutes that feel like a lifetime, I escape alive and intact, only my vocal cords injured. I ask Dahlia if we can sit on a nearby bench for a while.

"Being stuck in a cage, hurtling into the air out of control, that was my personal hell," I say, still panting.

"Aww, honey," she says. "I'm so sorry you hated it. You just got to learn to trust."

That evening, over greasy slices of pepperoni pizza in the camp cafeteria, Heather tries to convince me to join in on the last altar call.

"It's so awesome down there, you just have to try it. How come you haven't yet?" Heather asks.

"I don't know. I just don't," I say. I can't help but be a little suspicious by her sudden friendliness. Heather hardly talked to me this week. In fact, the only person who notices me is Dahlia. I am ready to go home and see Jane and tell her all about this weird camp.

"Well, I used to be lukewarm too," she says. "But then I met the Holy Spirit, thanks to Candace and Jessa. Ever since then, I just want more of Jesus. Don't you want more of Jesus?"

"What does lukewarm mean?" I ask.

"It means you're not hot for Jesus," she says. "Jessa talks about it a lot; I'm surprised you haven't heard her. Anyway, don't you want more of Jesus?"

Heather is eleven days older than me, but is talking to me like I am a little kid.

"Sure, more of Jesus would be great," I say.

"Well you won't get more of him without pressing in. Jessa has been wondering why you doodle in your notebook while the rest of us are meeting Jesus," she says. She is making smacking noises as she eats and talks, and I can see chewed up pieces of crust in her mouth.

When the Camp Lady summons us to the front to respond to the Call of Fire a few hours later, Heather squeezes my hand and pulls me out of my seat. I walk to the steps of the stage, ready to ask for more of God. *Dear God, please let me have more of you. Amen.*

"Holy fire! Holy fire! Consume us, Lord Jesus! Consume us, Father!" The crowd joins in on the Camp Lady's ad-libbed melody. My stupid prayer is lost in the chaos of prayers more loud and important than mine. Being in the middle of the commotion at the altar is even scarier than watching it from a distance. My heart pounds faster.

"Holy fire, Holy fire, Consume us," I sing along because there's nothing else to do. I raise my right hand, which is kind of the bare minimum I feel like I can get away with down here. Heather places her hand on my shoulder and prays over me.

"Jesus, just meet Carly tonight. Just meet her in this special place, Jesus," she whispers. "Thank you, Jesus, meet Carly tonight, Lord. Meet her tonight in this place." But I don't feel anything except a racing heart. The frizzy-haired, pimply girl is ahead of her time again, already rolling on the floor and screaming, while most of the other girls are still easing into the Jesus-y mood. She flops around inches from my ankles. I hope I don't accidentally step on her. I take a good look at her face, and I wonder if she was so close to the Holy Spirit, why she doesn't ask it to take away her acne. Then I think about what a cruel thing that is to think about someone, and I understand why the Holy Spirit doesn't seem to have any interest in me.

Candace, who usually spends altar calls praying over the other girls, is meeting the Spirit for herself this time. She had warned us of this earlier today. She said she had poured out so much that she felt spiritually dry, and needed to get filled up on the Spirit again. I watch her kneel on the floor on all fours, weeping and sticking her butt out to the music every fourth beat or so. I guess that's okay to do because there aren't any boys here.

Jessa comes over and taps Heather's shoulder.

"The Lord told me that the Spirit has something special for you tonight," I hear her say.

Heather glances at me, with that look of pity I keep seeing this week, and turns to face Jessa. Jessa puts both her arms around Heather, their faces inches apart. They start swaying and proclaiming a lot of things in Jesus's name, using big words like *breakthrough* and *victory* and *transcendence*. I think I feel something close to jealousy at this, although for what I am not sure.

The pimply girl's eyes jolt open and she looks right at me, or maybe right through me. "Goyoba-shet-ofana Honda-yoba!" She shouts. Then her eyes roll back into her skull. I have to get out of here.

Right now. I interrupt Heather and Jessa's prayer to tell Jessa I have a headache and am going to bed.

"I hope you feel better," Jessa says, and I can't decide if she is sympathetic or suspicious. I don't care at this point. I can't take it anymore. Heather looks at me, but only for a moment. Her face is glowing with anticipation for what might happen next.

Back in Pine Canyon, I grab my sleeping bag and teal knock-off JanSport backpack from the church van, chuck it in the trunk of Mom's car, and slip into the front seat without saying goodbye to anyone. I've never been so happy to be home.

Mom wants to hear about camp, but I don't feel like talking. How can I explain what I saw when I am not even sure myself?

"Did you have a good time?" Mom asks.

"Yeah, it was nice," I say.

"Nice? Well, was it fun?" she asks.

"Sort of," I say.

"How did the Crazy Slipper Contest go?" she says.

"It was great," I say. "But I didn't win. Some people really went all out."

Three

Summer camp turned out to be my social demise at Missionettes, and most of the girls ignore me now, more than they did before. Except for Candace, who is continually nice to me. She attends the musicals I perform in, and sometimes brings other girls from Missionettes, even though I can tell they don't want to be there. When the other girls are laughing at an inside joke from some party they all attended without me (this happens a lot), she changes the subject. Last week, the group took a trip to the Salvation Army Thrift Store as a reward for memorizing Scripture. I had to miss the trip because of a dress rehearsal for *Tom Sawyer: The Musical*. I am used to missing out by now.

"Let's go to the Salvy, just you and me," Candace says the next Wednesday at Missionettes, lightly punching my shoulder like we are buddies. The "Salvy" is Candace's hip nickname for the Salvation Army.

Maybe Candace wants to be friends with me, I think. *That would be so cool.* A smile spreads to my whole face.

Missionettes overall has been pretty disappointing for me. I only joined because Paul joined the Royal Rangers, the boy's club put on by Pine Canyon Assemblies of God Church. Paul went on camping and boating trips, worked for badges, and built strong bonds with his leaders—or "commanders" as he called them. It sounded cool, so I decided to try out the girl's counterpart. The girls, I quickly learned, do not do any of those things. There are no boat outings, camping trips, community service projects, or competitions to partake in. At the junior high level, we have weekly Bible studies on feminine topics. Still, the idea of belonging to a club excited me, so I paid Candace fifteen dollars for a three-ring binder with a shiny magenta butterfly on the cover. Our official handbook. I pored over that binder, reading all about purity, modesty, holiness, and the Spirit. For the last few months, we have been memorizing Psalm 139, reciting "You knit me together in my mother's womb" together each week. Candace and Jessa say the Psalm is about abortion, which they call Satan's Genocide.

My family is Christian, but not *serious* Christian, so all this is new to me. My parents are sporadic churchgoers, and my friends are a strange bunch of athletes, theater nerds, and fellow homeschoolers whom I met through group classes and field trips. I love my friends, but they are so scattered. They aren't a *group* like the girls at this church. I also have a feeling the church girls wouldn't approve of what my friends and I do for fun. At my fourteenth birthday party not too long ago, a few friends and I celebrated by filming a pretend commercial for "Turd Clippers." In the video, Jane hovers over the toilet with my dad's biggest pruning shears, shouting, "Rats! It's too big to flush again! Good thing I have my trusty Turd Clippers!" That was my cue to come in singing our Turd Clipper jingle. This escapade was inspired by a VHS copy of *The Best of Saturday Night Live Parody Commercials*, which I have already checked out from the library a dozen times so far this year. I watch it again and again, delighting in the glint in Phil Hartman's eye as he plays off his love for Colon Blow

Cereal so straight and sincere, and laugh until my stomach hurts watching Dan Aykroyd drop an entire fish into a blender during a breathy sales pitch for the Bass-o-Matic 76.

I know not to talk about these things in front of the Missionettes, so I quickly become known as "the shy one."

Candace grew up in the church and says her main passion is to help us girls mature into pure and godly women. She wears baggy jeans and sweatshirts most days because she is so committed to the principles of modesty. She isn't afraid to chastise us for the things we say and do that don't glorify the Lord. Though she never shows it, I know Candace has a secret lighter side, because once during a Missionettes sleepover at her apartment, I spotted the movie *Tommy Boy* on her dresser. She caught me looking at it and threw a shirt over it without saying anything. Chris Farley movies are definitely contraband at church.

Candace must conceal her weakness for potty humor, probably because she takes her role as our spiritual mentor seriously. Maybe I'll talk to her about my love for Chris Farley on our trip together. Maybe it will be our secret.

The following rainy Saturday morning, Candace and I make the fifteen-mile drive to the thrift store in the next town over, where I can spend five dollars on anything I want, my reward for memorizing all eighteen anti-abortion verses in Psalm 139. I scour the clothes looking for something trendy, perhaps a pair of flared jeans. After an hour rummaging through crowded racks of clothing, I settle on a pair of wide-leg khaki pants. Not as trendy as I hoped, but they will do. They are $1.20 over the spending limit and I have no money. Candace says that's okay and pulls out her wallet to cover the difference.

On the way home, I ask Candace what she wants for her nineteenth birthday, which is in two weeks.

"Well, I've asked my parents for something, but I know they can't afford it," she says.

"Yeah, like a million dollars?" I say, feeling clever.

"No, like new tires for my car," she says. Her voice is flat.

"Oh."

"I'll probably just have to keep saving. Maybe they can give me like fifty bucks toward them," she says.

I peer out the window in silence, feeling embarrassed and childish. Candace is a grown-up, with real grown-up problems, like how she will find the money to put tires on her car. It hits me that Candace isn't spending her Saturday driving thirty miles in the rain to buy me ugly pants because I am her friend—after all, I am seven years younger and a total nerd—but because I am a project in her ministry. A few miles pass by, and I tune into the sound of puddles sloshing underneath us. *Candace isn't my friend.* The realization doesn't hurt me the way I think it should. Instead, I am fascinated by whatever external force motivated Candace to spend her Saturday wearing out her tires with a girl like me. I wonder if this is the kind of thing someone does when they are under the influence of the Holy Spirit. I want to address Candace with my newfound knowledge that we are not friends, just to clear the air. But I don't, because I guess the entire premise of having a person as a ministry project only works when the project is tricked into thinking they are someone's friend. It would be better for me to play along with the Holy Spirit and not let on that I know why Candace is being so nice. After all, Candace is the only one who talks to me at church. I can't afford to lose her.

I keep going to Missionettes and remind myself that even if I have no friends, it shouldn't matter. According to the songs we sing at church, Jesus is supposed to be our best friend.

—

On a Wednesday night in late winter, I am standing in the sanctuary with my Missionettes club, a spattering of faithful Pentecostals, and a few Pine Canyon vagabonds. Pastor Frank is leading us in the chorus of a worship song. The smell of Dahlia's mom's pork-and-bean soup still wafts in the air. On Wednesday nights, Pine Canyon Assemblies of God opens their doors to anyone looking to feed their stomachs with homemade soup and store-bought French bread, and their souls with the Truth of the Word. It usually is only church people who turn up most weeks, but the homeless guy who came last week must have told his friends about the free soup and maybe Jesus too, because tonight there are three men in stained wool coats in the row across from me. Pastor Frank had sat with them at dinner and laughed his belly laugh at whatever it was they were telling him. Pastor Frank loves talking to outsiders—not me so much because I'm just a little girl—but the really heathen kind of outsiders he can bless and save.

The Missionettes are expected to attend the worship portion of adult church service before breaking off into our own group. I have asked why we have to do this several times when the Royal Rangers don't, and nobody can give me a legitimate reason. But the other girls seem to accept it, so I do too. I don't have a choice.

Usually sticking around for worship time isn't so bad, but there is one problem: we never know how long Pastor Frank will last. Sometimes it would be ten minutes, and then the handful of us Missionettes would funnel off to our closet-sized room to talk about the Bible while eating Hostess treats. But other times we'd be stuck in worship for forty minutes or more of singing, praying, and weeping.

Tonight, it is going on longer than ever. Everybody's eyes are closed and the Spirit must be moving, because they are singing extra loud, a song about Jesus being their lover and best friend.

Pastor Frank's voice barrels over everyone else's. "Let's sing just that line again."

"I will sing to you until the very e-hend. I sing to you until the very e-hend. I will sing to you until the very e-hend," the group repeats the line at least fifty times. I am beginning to worry they really will. I shift my weight to one leg and bend my knee. Nobody else seems bothered, even my peers, who look enraptured as they sing to Jesus. I guess I was wrong to assume they, like me, would much rather be munching on the cupcakes Candace made this week and sharing with each other about what God is teaching us, especially this week because our homework was to read the first chapter of a book called *And the Bride Wore White: Seven Secrets to Sexual Purity*. Talking about sex is always interesting, even if it is only about why we shouldn't have it.

Pastor Frank stretches his arms to the ceiling and marches around the room as he sings. His wife, Cindy, a woman with lots of eyeliner and short spiky black hair, plays the piano behind him. Everybody has their hands raised, and their bodies sway with the music, except for the two new homeless guys and me. They are standing stiffly, their arms folded, with big eyes and blank looks on their faces. But the original homeless guy is plenty enthusiastic to make up for the other two, shouting "Jesus!" and clapping at every beat.

Pastor Frank suddenly halts. Everyone stops singing. We wait. Eyes scrunched and arms outstretched, Pastor Frank begins to shout out a vision the Lord has given him. He starts pacing the room, his eyes still closed, delivering the Word. "God is moving a fresh revival among us, a sweet drink of his Spirit, in these last days. Grab on to the Spirit. Grab on!" he says.

"Yes, Jesus," moans a short woman in the row in front of me. I stare at the bald spot on the top of her bobbing head as she prays.

Cindy continues to play piano, improvising her music to match Pastor Frank's tone. As he shouts, she plays dissonant, eerie, and minor chords. I look over at Candace, hoping she would make a move to get us out of here and start our meeting, but she does not look back. She is mesmerized.

Pastor Frank cycles through a breadth of emotions in his Word. One minute he is angry, then he is sad. Then he is urgent and vigorous, before giving way to exuberance and ecstasy. And then he is quiet. I cross my arms and decide his delivery is excessive and tacky. He looks extra reptilian tonight, with his triple chin quaking with every word, long neck outstretched to the heavens, and eyes darting around his congregation. Like a spirit-filled Gila monster.

"The Spirit is breathing on us right now. Hear it, feel it, smell it. Oh, how sweet. . . ." His tirade melts into a moment of controlled, whispery tenderness. There are tears running down his cheeks in large, glistening streaks. Cindy's tense chord progression morphs into a gentle, tinkering backdrop of high notes. Not once does she look at the keys; her eyes are fixed on her husband. The Spirit must be speaking to her, too. An hour has gone by, and we are still standing. I start to suspect Pastor Frank is faking it, that maybe he is putting an endless string of words together because he likes the sound of his own voice. I like this better than having to wonder if the Holy Spirit is this boring and disrespectful of people's time. I feel guilty for thinking this and apologize to God for dissing his Holy Spirit.

"Amen," he finally says, and exhales, but his eyes are still closed. I think maybe we are set free. But Cindy continues playing music, now a swelling cascade of treble notes. *Stop playing the piano so he opens his eyes*, I think. *Stop enabling him to go on forever like this.* But the music goes on.

"Isn't the Lord such a sweet, sweet presence?" he asks, and the group nods and clucks.

No, I think. *No, it's not sweet. It's boring and weird.*

"Thank you, Jesus. Thank you, Jesus. Thank you, Jesus," he says. Instead of letting us go, his voice heats back up and he launches into another round of praying and Word giving, and the piano gets loud and dramatic again.

I hold my breath and feel like I might implode from boredom, and if that makes me ungodly, I don't care. I wish the Spirit would give Pastor Frank a more interesting, less repetitive Word. I have seen Pastor Frank get revved up before, but this is beyond anything rational. Who does he think he is, anyway? How dare he keep us in here like this for two hours! How selfish to think his words are the most important thing for us to hear. I bet I could sound profound too if I had endless musical accompaniment.

Finally, he ends, after one last prayer tirade. Candace has gathered us to the corner of the sanctuary and is passing out the cupcakes we were supposed to have during our meeting tonight along with permission slips for an upcoming sleepover.

"That was really long," I say, trying to evoke a reaction from Candace about what just happened.

"We are so blessed to have Pastor Frank who hears from the Lord," she says.

The other girls smile and agree. "Amazing," one of them chimes in. They are all on his side, I realize. I'm the only one. I'm the only one who thinks this is a problem. Maybe it is *my* problem.

I'm tired and cranky when Mom picks me up, and on the drive home I whine about how Pastor Frank held us hostage.

"That's very strange," she says. "But I'm sure that sweet pastor's wife will whisper to him sometime this week, 'Honey, those little girls didn't get to go to their Missionettes class,' and he'll make sure not to get carried away again."

"Hopefully," I say.

But something about the way Cindy was playing the piano tells me that would not be the case.

It's the day of the big move, the one Mom and Dad have been talking about ever since I can remember. *Abbey Road* is blasting on Paul's stereo, and Mom is laughing all these generous laughs at Dad's jokes, which she mainly ignores on most other days.

I carry a box of my clothes from my old room in the trailer to my new room in the Barn, mouthing the words to "Octopus's Garden."

"We should have hired movers," Dad says when we pass between trips.

"I know, it's so far! Too heavy, can't go on!" I say, holding my back.

"Hey, I have an idea. You tell your friends you moved, and when they ask for your new address, tell them it's the same as the old one. That'll confuse 'm!" Dad says.

Mom loads trays of silverware into the new kitchen and laughs at Paul's excitement to have a *real door* to his bedroom. In the trailer, Paul's room was an office nook without a door.

A part of me never thought this day would come. I'd heard about this plan my whole life, and now that it's happening, I don't quite believe it.

Over the years, I saw the Barn get new insulation and electrical wires and plumbing and a wood burning stove and new drywall. Some of it I helped with, like the puttying and sanding of nail dents in the drywall. The original Barn floor—wide plank redwood panels with knots and holes—is now caulked and sealed. The A-frame structure of the Barn is now a grand, high-ceilinged open home, with the kitchen and living area and fireplace and entryway all in one room. The eat-in kitchen has these big windows and faces the edge of the canyon and a rose garden Mom put in from bare roots last winter.

"I don't think I'll ever complain about doing dishes again," Mom says.

"Me neither," I say.

"Can you just picture this room with a Christmas tree?" she says.

I unpack my stuff in my new room, leaving behind whatever I don't want. It's not like the trailer is going anywhere. I picked this room in the Barn years ago when it was a storage closet full of rakes and rats—back in the days when we all dreamed about life in the Barn—because it made it easier to picture life there with a room picked out. As construction commenced, we built add-on rooms for the parents and Paul, but I held fast to the small, windowless room I'd chosen as a nine-year-old. I like that my room cost not much money to build—at my family's pace, picking this room could have shaved six months or more off the move-in date. Besides, I think it's the best room ever, even at fourteen. I set up a rose-tinted lamp with a bronze base shaped like vines. Without windows, I can have mood lighting any time of day.

The house is as beautiful and weird as you can imagine a house renovated from a barn on a tight budget. At twelve hundred square feet, it's not a big house, but it feels like a palace to us. Paul and I are giddy to have more space, to have a house with a wooden door like our friends. I can't wait to invite friends over, maybe even a few of the girls from church.

I'm happy, but Mom and Dad seem even happier. They are dancing around the Barn, now our *home*, and singing and kissing when they pass each other with their boxes of stuff. After years of fighting about the construction of this house, from the choice of ceiling fans to the choice of contractor Dad hired who drank beer on the job, they are dancing like they are in love, like maybe they weren't as happy in the trailer as they let on.

It doesn't matter, because we have a house now, and it's the coolest house I've ever seen.

Candace started inviting me to youth group a long time ago, and tonight I finally worked up the nerve to go. Youth group is different from the Missionettes, because boys are allowed, and older teens too, not just junior high kids. I'm fourteen, but I am still one of the youngest people here, which makes me feel even more awkward. Candace says I need to go to youth group because I've signed up to volunteer for an outreach the group is planning this summer called The Spot, and it is important for me to be unified in their vision for the event.

Everyone is dressed similarly: the girls in loose corduroys and modest, baggy T-shirts, and the boys in shorts and Quicksilver shirts. I am in a blue camouflage tank top I bought from a tent vendor at the Pine Canyon Fourth of July parade. Even though the church doesn't have air conditioning and gets sweltering in the summer, I wish I had worn a baggy T-shirt like the other girls. Next time I'll remember this, I tell myself. Slowly and clumsily, I am learning how to be a good Christian.

Heather gives me a hug.

"Cute haircut, sweetie," she says.

I think I am supposed to give her a compliment now. I think that's how this works. She is waiting for me to say something. I've got to think of something, quick. Would it be weird if I complimented

her on her teeth? Yeah, that would be weird. She might think I'm
making fun of her, because they aren't particularly good teeth. I like
them because they're unique. Crap. Now I've waited too long and it's
too late to say anything, even "thank you." So I stare at her without
saying anything, and she looks at me funny and goes back to talking
to Mark, who doesn't acknowledge my presence at all. I blew my first
night at youth group within thirty seconds of my arrival.

Some of the other girls from Missionettes are here, but they are
busy talking to other people. Everyone is talking to other people,
and I don't know how to seamlessly enter a conversation, and what
would I say to them if I did? I can only hover around different conversations—standing near people and trying to laugh at the right
moments—for so long before I wish I could disappear into a cloud
of smoke.

I decide sitting in the corner looking painfully uncomfortable
is easier than trying too hard and still looking painfully uncomfortable, so I make my way over to a stack of padded chairs in the back of
the room. I study the sanctuary's stained maroon carpet to pass the
time. My eyes get lost in the galaxy of green stains and brown stains
and yellow bleach marks. Another wave of laughter rolls through the
group. No, they aren't laughing at me. They don't even see me.

Jessa starts playing piano and asks everyone to gather around the
youth pastor, James, who is leaving Pine Canyon for another ministry.
I glance at the clock. We are an hour behind schedule already, and
we haven't even started. This might be a late night. I have never met
James before tonight, so I feel pointless being at his goodbye service.
I probably should just go home now, I think, as I encircle James at the
altar with everyone else.

"Let's ask God to anoint James with the Power of the Holy Spirit,"
Jessa says. Oh no. Anointing and power. It's one of those prayer times.

I keep quiet, one hand extended toward James and the other in my pocket.

"Lord, we ask that you would fill James with your blood," prays Jacob, who is now engaged to Jessa. "That through your blood, James would walk in power in his new ministry, that he would stomp on the demonic influences that try to squelch your Spirit, that he would start an unstoppable fire in a lukewarm church, that a revival in this generation of lip-service Christians would start with him." James is taking a job at a Lutheran church.

These are not the kind of "Dear God, thank you for (fill in the blank), please (fill in the blank), amen," prayers I am well versed in, the prayers I pray with Grandma and sometimes Mom. This is a special language everyone here but me is fluent in. How did they learn to speak in all these gorgeous poetic phrases? How do they come up with these flowing metaphors on the spot? I wonder. That knot in my stomach I remember from camp starts to rise up again.

Fueled by the "Yes, Lords" and moans from the group, Jacob's prayer grows more intense. Like a car that moves faster and faster until it spins out of control, the group's prayers are gaining energy, and then something strange happens, even for this group. Their voices reach this height in volume and intensity, and then the bubble breaks, like a climax, and the group shatters into tiny pieces of quiet moans and whimpers and whispers in nonsensical babbles.

I hear the roar of a vehicle approaching from outside, and it sounds like Dad's van pulling into the driveway. What if he is here to pick me up? My father drives a giant white utility van to transport his painting equipment to and from jobs. While Mom does most of the chauffeuring for my brother and me, Dad occasionally picks us up from activities in the evenings after work. I love rides in Dad's van, where I score pieces of spearmint gum and flip through his books of color swatches. He always apologizes for the mess, but I never mind. I love seeing pieces of his world—paint chips, brushes, names and phone numbers scratched in pencil on the back of sandpaper—all over the seat, the floor and the dashboard, pieces I can touch and smell and live in for the duration of our drive.

The Pine Canyon church people are always telling me Dad needs to be saved. I think they say this because he grew up Catholic and would rather read the Sunday paper than go to a Sunday service. They tell me I play an important role in saving my dad from the fiery pits of hell. Okay, so maybe they don't say that outright, but I know what they mean when they ask me with those sad eyes if my dad is the spiritual leader of my family. I've been thinking, and my plan to save Dad is to appeal to his logic by showing him that born-again Christians are sensible, hardworking people just like him.

I cannot let him see what is going on in youth group. What if he pops inside, eager to see what my new activity is all about? I can picture it. He'd stand in the doorway, crossing his muscular, paint-speckled arms, darting his eyes around. He'd see Jacob thrashing from his hips and crying and begging Jesus to break the chains of the enemy. I bet he hasn't seen anything like this before. He might do something really loud and embarrassing, like shout, "What in the world is going on here? I thought this was supposed to be Sunday school!" Or he might come try to give me a hug in front of everyone and ask me if I want to leave (which I do, desperately, but how embarrassing would that be?). Or he might just stand there in the doorway, taking it all in. No matter the outcome, it would do some real damage in the way of Operation Get Dad Saved.

The frenzy around me at the altar is escalating again. They are building to another climax, from the sound of it. Pastor James is on all fours crying and everyone is hovered over him. The rumbling outside is still going on. Dad must be leaving his car running, waiting for me. I have to stop him from coming in. I back away from the group slowly, and then turn and run through the sanctuary. I bolt through the church double doors, and tear into the parking lot where I plan to jump in Dad's van and be taken away from this place forever. My heart is pounding out of my chest. Only I don't see any van. I check the parking lot and look up and down Grove Street. No paint van, no Dad. I collapse on the gravel and broken concrete parking lot near an overgrown blackberry bush and begin to cry.

I cry because I am frightened for the way my peers pray, and I'm angry I can't pray like them. I cry because I didn't know how to compliment Heather when I was supposed to, and because, like a socially inept freak, I watched the group mingle from a distance for forty-five minutes before service started. I cry because I knew all along that the rumbling noise was a train chugging across town, and I just so wanted to believe in something else. I cry because I don't think I believe in the Holy Spirit.

I pause between sobs for a moment and notice the sturdy blackberry vines next to me and their thick thorns. I take a deep breath of still mountain air. That the earth remains unmoved by my outburst somehow eases my anxiety. I remember to breathe. I reach out and pick a berry, hard and red. It is blackberry season and the vines on the riverbanks a few miles away are heavy with ripe and juicy berries—Mom made a pie from them yesterday. But the ones here don't get enough water so they stay red all summer before shriveling up on the vine in September. I pop the berry in my mouth and suck on it, piercing sections of it with my teeth and letting its bitterness spread down my throat.

I can still hear Jessa playing the piano from here. I relax into the music a bit and realize from out here, it almost sounds pretty.

Occasionally, I hear a muffled shout, but from this distance, it doesn't scare me.

"Yes, Lord," I mumble.

"Yes, Jesus." It sounds strange coming off my tongue.

"Yes, Holy Spirit." I practice the melodic, monotone inflection they use. "Jesus."

It is time for me to go back inside. I stand up. "Yes Lord."

I walk to the pale blue metal church door. "Yes, Jesus."

I rest my hand on the knob for a moment. "Yes, Holy Spirit."

I open the door. "Jesus."

I join Heather and Jessa and Jacob and everyone else, who are still huddled around James. Nobody looks up, like they hadn't even noticed I was gone. I extend my hands. "Yes, Lord," I say, quietly, and a rush of energy surges through me. Is this how it feels? I wonder. "Yes, Looord," and this time, I extend my vowels the way they did. "Yes, Looord," a little louder yet.

I realize if I concentrate on saying *Yes, Lord* or *Jesus* every fifteen seconds or so, praying with this group isn't so scary. I am focusing on the words coming from my own mouth, how they sound on my tongue, how they make me feel, how I wonder if God is hearing me say them.

"Holy Spirit," I whisper, this time under my breath so only I can hear. *I'm ready.*

Worship at Pine Canyon Assemblies of God scares me a little less each week I expose myself to it. I am able to attend Missionettes and youth group without being frightened, and I've even relaxed enough to get into planning The Spot, passing out fliers around town and practicing a worship dance routine to perform with the other girls. When the night of The Spot finally arrives, I think I even feel excited.

Our fliers must have worked because there is a crowd of at least a hundred people here. There is a bounce house to my left and a rousing game of inflatable sumo wrestling to my right. Christian rock blasts from the amplifiers all around. Teenagers with eyebrow piercings are slurping free snow cones. I feel important for helping put on an outreach so big. Jacob is standing on a stage the elders of the church hand-built for the event. He's crying.

"My life was empty and sad. I was always out looking for my next high," he says. Some people are listening (mostly people from youth group) but most of our guests are too busy playing to pay attention. "I was high on 'shrooms. A sixteen-year-old young man, dead to himself already. It's how the world lives, isn't it? Dead in spirit. So anyway, I'm high on 'shrooms, and I go to the roller skating rink. The lights are dimmed, and those little white lights that look like fireflies are dancing everywhere. I watched those lights spin around, and the lights morphed into a rink full of people living empty lives," he says. He pauses, like the words pain him to say.

"I audibly heard the voice of the Lord that night. He said 'Jacob, you have a destiny that is brighter than all these people, if you surrender yourself to me.' And I fell on the floor, in the midst of all these people and dancing lights, sobbing. The Lord cleared my head and *bam*! I became instantly sober," he says, snapping his fingers into the microphone. "I gave my heart to the Lord right there on the floor of that roller skating rink, and I never did drugs again."

"Praise Jesus, that's my man!" Jessa says, from the left side of the stage. Jacob doesn't break focus.

"I now live in the Secret Place of the Lord and I would never, ever go back. God gave me a calling that night, and I live every day for him. God longs for you, too. God is moaning and longing for your heart. God is pursuing you like a jealous lover. And that God, the Living God of the Universe, is here tonight."

Jacob stands in silence for a few minutes, and then nods to Kevin, the sound guy. Kevin pushes up his thick, cracked glasses and gives a thumbs-up sign. Kevin is older than most the kids at youth group but hangs around anyway. He takes his volunteer job as the sound guy seriously, even saving his own money to buy equipment for the church. I can't help but think he probably should save for a car instead, since he can't even take his 1960s Thunderbird on the freeway because it doesn't go fast enough. All of his shirts are the kind sold in a bag. Kevin presses a few buttons, and a beat comes from the speakers. Jacob begins bopping his head, subtle at first and then jerkier. Then he dives to the floor on his elbows and whips his legs above his head around in a circle, and then another circle in a breakdance move. His biceps bulge like Popeye as they work to suspend his whole body. He's dancing all over the stage, and people from the sumo wrestling game and the bounce house begin to file to the foot of the stage to watch. A couple of guys I don't recognize jump on the stage and breakdance with him, all of them with biceps like Jacob's. One of them takes off his shirt to reveal a whole torso of Popeye muscles. I'm not sure what this has to do with Jacob's testimony, but it's pretty awesome. I glance at Jessa, who is beaming at her fiancé. People are clapping to the beat and hooting and hollering. Jacob does a move with both of his legs straight up in the air, and then jumps off the stage and dumps a bottle of water over his head, shouting, "Yeah Jesus!" People are giving him hugs and high fives and telling him he's got a "sick beat."

Candace takes the stage as the ruckus is barely dying down. "And now, we will see a worship dance from the Missionettes group," she says. The audience isn't listening. How we can follow that act with our little sign language dance, I have no idea. We have been practicing our routine for months and praying the Holy Spirit would touch someone through us. This is our moment; although now I'm thinking we should have opened for the breakdancing-shroom-testimony-show, not the other way around. I walk on stage with Heather, Dahlia, Krissy, and Amanda, and pose with my head down and arms at my side, just like we practiced. As I look down, I notice I'm the only one wearing shorts. The other girls are wearing long pants or long skirts. I guess I missed the unspoken dress code again. The bright pink denim shorts I'm wearing came from a recent shopping trip to the junior's department at JC Penney's with Mom. I rarely shop in the juniors' section, because I am still small enough to fit into the larger kid sizes, which are a lot cheaper. But Mom said these shorts were a special purchase for the beginning of summer. I love them so much I only take them off to wash them, so I didn't even think about wearing anything else tonight.

No time to think about it now—the sound guy presses play on our chosen CD, and our beautiful bongo intro to the Third Day song, "Your Love, Oh Lord," begins.

I reach my hands in the air in a flowing, swooping motion right on the beat.

The song is all about metaphors of God's love in the mountains and sky and oceans. I groove my hands in the shape of a mighty cascading mountain as we had practiced, making sure to only move my upper body and plant my feet on the ground. I remember what Candace said—we are trying to lead people to Jesus, not our hips.

I swirl my hands around in the motion of a powerful ocean wave and stop thinking about our dance moves as I let them flow through me naturally. I close my eyes and mouth the words and move to the rhythm of the bongos. The audience and the other Missionettes fade away. I am freely dancing with God now, the one I've known my whole life, the God who flows in rivers and makes tall trees and who fills my lungs. The God who is in amazing books and my grandmother's hugs and Mom's blackberry pie. I'm flying in the shadow of God's wings, experiencing God's untamable love and feeling it overflow to the deepest parts of me. The song ends, my hands are held in the air, and I'm so absorbed in my own world, I barely hear the audience clapping. When I open my eyes and come back to reality, I look down and to my horror, I see my shorts are unbuttoned and my fly is unzipped. This is like one of those terrifying naked-in-public dreams, only real. I quickly zip up as I shuffle off stage, looking around to see if anyone is watching. Was my fly down the whole time? Did anyone see my yellow cotton underwear? *I'm such a stupid klutz*, I think. *Nobody noticed. It's not a big deal. Don't be embarrassed.* But my feet keep going, in a direction away from all these people, toward a juniper bush across the parking lot that looks like such a cozy place to hide.

Candace reaches out and pulls on my arm. "Where are you going?" she asks.

"I, um, don't know," I say, rubbing my arm. Her grab didn't hurt, but it startled me.

"Well, not so fast. I have something I need to tell you," she says. My mouth turns dry. I can tell by her voice she's not happy.

"I'm listening," I say, dreading what was about to come out of her mouth.

"That was very inappropriate," she hisses. "Your shorts were unbuttoned almost the whole time. It's bad enough that you were wearing shorts, but then to leave your fly down? Were you trying to be sexy or something?"

"I'm so sorry. I didn't know," I whisper. I look around to see if anyone can hear us. People are too busy laughing and talking to notice us, thankfully.

"Then why were you moving your hips around like Britney Spears?" she says.

"Oh," I say. I'm thinking a thousand different things, but "Oh" is all that comes out. I want to tell her I didn't mean to look like Britney Spears, that I was dancing in the shadow of God's wing, but I'm so embarrassed all I can do is look at the ground. Candace's frown softens and she draws a deep breath.

"I know you are really good at performing in plays and that's just your personality, but this is not the time or place for that." She starts again with a tired, teaching voice, "When we make things about us and our bodies, we block the Holy Spirit from moving in people's lives."

"I guess that makes sense," I say. Maybe I *was* trying to draw attention to myself. Maybe that wasn't really God I felt in the song. I don't know anything for sure anymore.

"Don't worry, I still really like you," she says, offering me a side hug, and I sense she means it. "I challenge you to a sumo wrestling match!"

I let out a sigh of relief at how quickly Candace forgave me as we walk arm in arm toward the wrestling arena. Our laughter fills the air all the way up to the moon that lights our path. There's a tiny jump in my heart. I can follow the rules if it means this.

Four

On a spring Friday, I use the driver's license I've had for two weeks to drive my brother and me to church for our first youth conference with Pine Canyon Assemblies of God. I'm sixteen now and feel so cool in Mom's stick shift Honda Accord. I'm the only girl my age I know who learned to drive on a manual transmission, and I feel like it makes me edgy. We blast Christian rock music from the car's cassette player and roll down all the windows. Today is the day of the youth conference, the day we've been waiting months for.

After arriving at the church, we wait. We always wait for hours when we meet at the church before an outing because Jacob doesn't like to plan things ahead of time. This used to bother me because it meant more time for awkward small talk, or to sit by myself in the corner. But these days, I can hang out at church all day because it means I get to be with Danny.

I met Danny a few months ago on a Wednesday night. I was sitting at a table by myself waiting for the service to begin when a guy with carrot-orange hair opened the door and slouched slightly to fit through it. He had a huge grin on his face, and he was looking around the sanctuary with big, wondrous eyes as if he were Alice arriving in Wonderland. He walked into the middle of the room. His grin didn't fade, even as he stood alone for a few seconds. He was at least a head taller than everyone else at church, and it seemed nobody had noticed him yet. I was working up the nerve to introduce myself when Pastor Frank himself lumbered up to him.

"Welcome to Pine Canyon Assemblies of God Church," Frank said, giving the man a vigorous handshake. "Name?"

"Danny. Danny McKeller," the man said.

"I'm glad you're here, Danny McKeller. What leads you here tonight?" Pastor Frank said.

"Well, I haven't been living for the Lord, and then Jesus came to me in a dream and said 'Serve Me.' So I figured I better listen," Danny said.

"Praise the Living God," Pastor Frank said, and then laughed like a child. I got the feeling that these are the moments he lives for as a pastor. Several other church members came to introduce themselves to Danny and pretty soon he had a small crowd around him as he shared his testimony. I listened without getting up.

"I was at Cal Poly, but I failed my classes because I was partying every night. I had to drop out," he said. The crowd gasped. "But that's all behind me now. I'm here to learn how to obey the Lord." He used all of himself when he spoke, waving his long, lanky arms around and widening his giant green eyes. I pretended to read my Bible but was watching him out of the corner of my eye. If he was in college, that meant he was at least eighteen—but he had this baby face that made him look twelve.

People around him wiped tears from their eyes and hugged him. "Danny, we hope you find a home here, and a home in Jesus," one woman said. His adoring crowd dispersed to clean up from dinner. Dahlia's mom served him some split pea soup in a Styrofoam bowl with a slice of French bread on top. He thanked her, and started to make his way my direction. I panicked and buried my nose further into the book of Isaiah. He was looking right at me, I could feel it, but I didn't look up.

"I knew a lot of pretty girls at college, but man, none of them are as full of life as the ones right here. I've been here like ten seconds and I already can tell you girls just have Jesus radiating out of you," he said, motioning to me and then around the room. "Who knew?"

Was he talking about me? I wasn't used to being called pretty, and definitely no boy had ever told me I was "full of life" before. I didn't know what to say. I wondered if he knew I was only fifteen. Everyone said I looked older. "What you reading?" he asked, and tore a bite off his bread.

"Oh, uh, the book of Isaiah," I said. "I just love how God proves himself faithful to the Israelites over and over again."

Danny started laughing, and I thought he was making fun of me. I'm such a nerd.

"This is like a dream. This amazing girl is telling me about God's Word," he said. "Pinch me."

I don't question where Danny McKeller came from, or how he washed up in this tiny church in this tiny town. God works in mysterious ways, I always hear other people saying. I am starting to believe that myself. I decided in that moment that wherever Danny was, that's where I wanted to be.

So now, three months later, I walk into the sanctuary with a little swagger, knowing this weekend will be exciting no matter what. I steal a peek at Danny and grin, and then I toss my sleeping bag and pillow in the pile with all the others. Danny sees me do this and dives into the pile like a cat pouncing on its prey.

"I'm the sleeping bag king!" he shouts, sprawling his long body over the mound of sleeping bags. Turns out Danny is twenty-one, but he plays like a kid—a kid who is not going to get away with being the sleeping bag king, if I have anything to say.

"No way! This is a democracy!" I pull sleeping bags from under him and scatter them around the room.

The others in the group agree with the idea of democracy, and to protect Danny from reigning, we each guard a sleeping bag. Danny sneaks around us, trying to snatch up unwatched sleeping bags for his kingdom. I chuck one at Danny's face and the game spirals out of control. We all start attacking each other with sleeping bags and pillows until we get so tired of laughing and throwing things that we collapse on our backs to catch our breath. Jacob and Jessa are in the church office with the door shut, so we can get away with lying on the floor in mixed company. With my back flat on the carpet and my face pointed up toward a dusty church ceiling fan, I realize this is the first time this group has seen Wild Child. I smile and wonder if I can be myself at church after all.

It's raining hard outside when we are ready to leave, and our luggage gets drenched as we carry it to the cars. Jacob is standing in the rain, counting kids and counting open seats in the cars we've planned to take, and realizes we are short a car.

"Some of us might have to double buckle," Jacob says.

"Not happening. I'll drive!" Danny says, and Jacob looks relieved.

I hop into Danny's car instead of the church minivan Jessa is driving or the SUV driven by a mother of one of the youth group boys. Danny's car will be the most fun, obviously. As we pull away in Danny's dented gold Geo Prizm, he tells us his windshield wipers are broken. "People don't really *need* windshield wipers," he says, laughing.

"Then how do you see out the window when it's raining?" I say. As a new driver, I am very fresh up on road safety laws. I think I was the only kid in my driver's education class who actually listened. I realize I need to tone down the nerdiness if I am going to look cool in front of Danny.

"Well, what windshield wiper companies don't want you to know is if you wait long enough, the rain falls off on its own," he says. "Here, I'll show you!" The road ahead is blurry and distorted through the layer of thick water on the glass, and it makes me nervous. But I laugh with him anyway. Those crooked windshield wiper companies are ripping everyone off! As we weave through downhill traffic on the interstate, the throng of pine and cedar trees gives way to sparse shrubs and dry oaks, and finally to nothing but the occasional cypress or palm tree in the flat, congested suburbs of Sacramento.

Jessa and Jacob, who are married now, and the new youth pastors at Pine Canyon Assemblies of God, have been praying for us for weeks to receive what God might have for us at this conference.

"What do you think this preacher is like?" I ask Danny. The three boys in the backseat are talking about some video game.

"I don't really know, but Jacob says he will have some divine appointments for us. I looked him up on the internet. He's a pretty famous preacher with an amazing anointing," he says.

"Cool," I say. I am still learning what words like anointing mean. Danny has picked up on the lingo way faster than me.

We pull up at Sonshine Church, a modern brick building with a huge white cross mounted on a tower, a smoothly paved parking lot, and a glistening green lawn big enough to play soccer on. It is the glitziest place of worship I have ever seen.

"Let's give a *woot* for Jesus for getting us here safely," Danny says, clapping his hands.

"*Woot!*" we all say.

—

"O Nazirite generation, arise! The Lord is raising up an army of people willing to separate themselves from this sinful culture in a vow of extreme devotion to God," the preacher shouts from the stage.

I watch in awe. He is a bald man of slight stature, wearing his Levi's high on the waist and held up with a thick leather belt. A prickly brown mustache is a parting curtain for a mouth full of crooked yellow teeth. He reminds me of some of the old guys who beg me for a quarter at the Greyhound Station next door to the Chinese restaurant where we have lunch after church on Sundays. If I had seen this man at the Greyhound station, I might have felt sorry for him and given him a quarter. But as he preaches, rhythmically swaying forward and backward over and over again, I know there is nothing to pity about him. He has what we all want: the Spirit of God in his words.

"May you burn for God more than you burn in lust for this world! Oh God of Israel, arouse your jealousy for the Nazirite generation," he says, lurching back and forth, punctuating each word and resting on each S sound.

The tension in my stomach comes back, but I remember something Jacob said about how the Spirit of God should make us uncomfortable. I breathe deep and push down the fear.

"Abayishanada shandawanda abayishi," the preacher says into the microphone. I know what speaking in tongues sounds like now, but the preacher's voice itself is scary, so scratchy and guttural, like slabs of granite dragged on pavement, like one of those crazy TV wrestling announcers. Hands from all over the audience shoot up in the air in his direction, and the room rumbles with the murmurings of "Yes, Lord" and "Jesus." I watch how the preacher moves. His feet are planted firmly on the ground, his legs spaced a foot apart, giving him a strong foundation for his thrusting upper body. "If you're a little freaked out, a little scared of the way I rock when the Holy Spirit moves through me, you better get used to it. The Spirit does a lot more crazy things than that! This is a physical taste of what will be rocked in the heavens today," he says.

His words break off into a wheezy laugh, and the laugh grows louder and louder. Now he is laughing and rocking and shouting hallelujah all at the same time. The crowd starts to laugh and shout hallelujah too. I sit still, taking everything in. Danny, who is next to me, is clapping and rocking in his seat. The preacher is talking about a mystical faith I have never known before, using words like *supernatural, miracles, prophecy,* and *radical devotion.* Pastor Frank talks about the supernatural too, but not like this. This is on another level.

He is telling a story of how he once was midway through preaching a word from the Lord when he realized he had a piece of snot dangling from his nose. I put down my pen. As far as I can remember, you weren't supposed to talk about snot in church. I got in trouble at my Baptist Sunday school when I was eight years old for doodling a picture on a tithing envelope of the devil with snot dripping down his chin. I thought it was so funny, I couldn't contain my giggles and I passed it to some of my classmates, who also thought it was hilarious. My Sunday school teacher grabbed the envelope from me and made me sit in the corner for the remainder of her lesson. She said my picture made Jesus sad. But here is a grown man, telling us from the pulpit that slimy nasal fluids can unlock heavenly powers. I am blown away. Maybe faith is more than just about being good. Maybe faith is about power.

"The Lord told me clearly and audibly, 'If you love me, let the snot dangle.' So I let that snot hang there as I preached for three hours, and let me tell you, the Lord shook things in the heavenly realm that night," the preacher says.

He says he got so deep in the things of the Spirit that he forgot the snot was there until it dripped onto his foot. Then another ball of snot formed, and it dangled for a good long while until that one dripped too.

"So if a piece of snot is hanging off my nose today, you'll know that the Spirit is about to come down mightily," he says.

Danny claps his hands and shouts. "*Woot! Woot!*"

Letting a piece of snot dangle in front of an audience is not for the faint of heart, I know that much. Maybe that act of humility—of extreme sacrifice—really could unleash spiritual powers. I know from youth group lessons that God honored boldness. But snot? With the crowd fired up, the preacher flips through the tissue-thin pages of his Bible like he is about to start a lesson. But then, as if he suddenly changed his mind, he shuts the Bible and closes his eyes. I wait along with a silent, expectant room. He reaches his hand out toward the crowd and mutters words too low for the microphone to pick up. Then he looks up and begins to speak.

"There is someone in this room, a young lady," he is talking slowly and deliberating over every word. "She is hiding something." He marinates in more silence for a good twenty seconds as all of us teen girls shift uncomfortably in our seats. "The Lord is telling me an evil spirit is twisting your thoughts . . . Satan has really gotten under your skin . . . I am getting a clearer picture now . . .The Lord is saying you have an eating disorder," he says. He pauses again, and raises his hands. My eyes bulge. I have never seen the Spirit reveal anything so specific—or juicy. Pastor Frank's prophecies are always about obeying the Lord because revival is coming. As far as I know, God never tells Pastor Frank anything exciting like people's secret eating disorders. "If you are that girl, I'd like you to come forward," he says.

A girl who looks no older than fourteen makes her way from her seat to the stage. I have never seen a girl with an eating disorder in real life before, at least not one that I knew about. She looks normal to me, not fat or skinny. I wonder if she is the type to starve herself or purge, or both.

The preacher flicks his wrist and a few female youth leaders come forward. They all lay hands on the girl. "We shake the power of evil that has caused this sickness in this young woman," he says.

"Yes Lord," several people in the crowd moan. Danny extends his arms in the direction of the girl.

"We cut ties with Satan and free this young lady right now. We claim deliverance from demonic voices. In Jesus's name, we claim wholeness right now," the preacher says. "In Jesus's name. In Jesus's name. In Jesus's name," he continues. His voice grows with intensity, and he begins screaming God's name, and the crowd whistles and claps. The girl is sobbing and whacking her hands against her chest as the preacher prays. The women circling her rock her back and forth and then they push her to the ground, where she thrashes like a fish on a stringer. They cover her with a blanket and stroke her forehead as she cries.

"In Jesus's name," the preacher says one last time before opening his eyes and scanning the audience. "Whew, the Spirit is powerful. Releasing *chains* tonight. Healing *people* tonight."

This is the first miracle I've seen. I stare at my lap. This kind of healing isn't provable—I would like to see someone grow a limb or something—but I guess that's me doubting the Holy Spirit again. I have to learn to have more faith.

I look up and see the preacher staring right at me. My heart starts beating fast and I can feel sweat beads forming in my armpits. I lock eyes with him and let him read my face. I get this creepy feeling he is watching my whole life unfold in this one gaze, even my secret thoughts. I feel a scary tickle down my spine. As much as I dread being exposed, I long to be known. I long to be discovered. I wonder what he knows.

"The Spirit is telling me there is someone here who battles the Spirit of Insecurity," the preacher says, not breaking eye contact with me. "I have a special word for you tonight if you come forward." I feel a tug at my heart, and I wonder if this is what people mean when they talk about being prompted by the Holy Spirit. I know this special word is for me and I need to receive it. But as much as I want to run to the stage and let the prayer ladies hold me as I cry, my muscles are locked. I can't move.

This could be the night everything changes, the voice says, and I feel myself tearing up. *Get up there.* But my body is frozen.

As I waver, a girl from the back walks down the aisle. She is crying too. I half expect the preacher to stop her and tell her to get back to her seat because the special word was for the girl in the glasses in row three. But he doesn't. He lays his hands on her shoulders and begins to prophesize over her passionately as I remain in my seat, crushed. Maybe he wasn't looking at me after all.

Jealousy wells up inside me for the girl who went up instead of me. I watch her flowing, long brown hair swish around her back as the preacher prays for her. Her hair is like Courtney Cox's and mine is so thin I have to wrap a rubber band around it three times to make a ponytail stay. I guess you can have great hair and still be insecure. Or maybe she stole my prophecy.

"Spirit of Boldness, take this young woman tonight. Let her respond to the call to be possessed by God," the preacher wails.

I close my eyes and absorb every word of the prayer. Meanwhile, the girl healed of her eating disorder is passed out and motionless on the floor by the preacher's feet. This is the last time I will miss out on something God has for me.

With the room captivated by the miracles, the preacher begins to present our special calling.

"I stand in a prophetic moment now, that a new breed of prophet is coming forward, an angelic release. America will see her Nazirites arise!"

I'm not really sure what he means by all this, but the crowd loves it. "Amen! Preach it! Hallelujah! Shondalay hondalay!" they say. He gets his Bible out and reads from the book of Numbers. The Nazirites were a group of people chosen by God to restore righteousness to Israel, it says. They followed rigid rules to find favor from God and to set themselves apart from the idolatrous culture around them. The Nazirites were instructed by God not to cut their hair, drink alcohol, or touch anything dead.

I have never heard about the Nazirites before in my sporadic Sunday school upbringing. I take frantic notes to keep up with the sermon. The other people from youth group nod along like they already know all of this. I have a lot of catching up to do.

The two most famous Nazirites in the Old Testament are Samson and Samuel, the preacher says. Samson was said to have acquired superhuman strength from his Nazirite vow, which all fell apart when Delilah cut his hair in probably the most dramatic haircut tale in history. Samuel was a Jewish prophet who was said to have gotten into big trouble with God when he broke his Nazirite vow by throwing a drinking party and touching a dead body. I understand why someone would want to have a drinking party because some of my friends like to do that, but I don't get why anyone would be tempted to touch a dead body. The Bible is full of weird stuff, I think.

The preacher also says that John the Baptist was a Nazirite.

John the Baptist fasted, baptized people, ate locusts, and abstained from wine, all to prepare the world for Jesus Christ's arrival. The preacher says the spirit of John the Baptist could enter any of us, possess us, and cause us to change the world. I hope I won't have to eat any bugs.

Spit flies out of the preacher's mouth and his bald head glistens as he scans the crowd. He acts like he is about to reveal something. We wait.

He says God came to him in a dream and told him to enlist a second coming of the Nazirites, a movement of young people who will submit to the Spirit of Separation and restore the United States to its moral foundations, to prophesize and burn the hearts of the rebellious. He says the modern day Nazirites need to rise up to fulfill this prophecy or else Jesus won't come back, and we definitely want Jesus to come back so the rapture can happen. When Jesus comes back, he will rescue Christians from the destruction of the world.

One stage light is shining over the preacher in an otherwise dark sanctuary. People to my left and right, teenagers thirsty for revival, raise their hands and mimic his rocking.

"Break off apathy, you men and women called to be prophets but who are numbed by the Spirit of Evil! Other teens can enjoy the pleasures of this life, but you are preparing for the pleasures of an inward fire that burns!" *What does the inward fire feel like?* I wonder. I want to feel it burn.

The preacher warns that the "harassment of Delilah"—seemingly harmless recreation such as sports, movies, and technology, or idols such as intellectualism, careers, and relationships—can neuter our hearts for God, just as Delilah debilitated Samson by taking a razor to his long hair.

I start to think about what might be neutering my heart for God.

If what the preacher is saying is true, then cutting out *Saturday Night Live* would be a small price to pay to see signs and wonders. Perhaps I am one or two steps away from seeing God move in my life. Maybe the world of the prophetic is just on the other side of a doorknob waiting to be turned. If so, I don't want to miss out over a few worldly pleasures. All my hobbies feel trivial when I think about this.

God, I'm sorry for letting Delilah harass me. Help me break off from the spirit of this world.

"Oh God of Israel, release your prophets to confront the Antichrist systems that bind this nation!" the preacher shouts.

I listen, shocked, as he tells us God came to him in a vision and told him that *Roe v. Wade* would be overturned through the Nazirites. Just as God instructed the Old Testament Nazirites not to touch anything dead, the modern day prophets would rise up against and overcome the spirit of death in our baby-killing culture. We would make history, and it would all point to God.

I glance down at my cherry-red Vans sneakers and intentionally mismatched socks, one white with Minnie Mouse on the outside ankle, and one purple plaid. A countercultural movement full of signs and wonders sounds like a lot of fun. I love the idea of being on a team doing something important for God. This is my chance to be a part of something powerful, something special. What if we really did make history? I look around at my youth group, this cluster of people I am beginning to call my own: my brother, looking up at the stage with wide eyes; the goofy boys close to his age, sitting on their hands so as not to fidget; my beautiful newlywed youth pastors, sitting close and writing spiritual nuggets in their notebook that they would probably later discuss by candlelight at home in between soft kisses; two of the girls I went to summer camp with three years ago, heads bowed and hands open. Can I commit to this task with these people?

And then I turn and steal a glance at Danny, who is wooting and dancing next to me.

I can definitely commit to this.

"Release the Nazirites all over the world, men and women who are called to be possessed by God," the preacher hisses, and I lift my hands, one at a time.

Possess me, God. Possess me.

The worship band files on stage and begins strumming their guitars with urgency. "Take us to the threshing floor tonight. Separate the precious from the vile. Our hearts are an altar and your love the flames. Oh Lord, the hour of prophecy is here!" the preacher says. I pray, joining my voice with an army of teens moaning for the Spirit of God.

Yes, Lord.
Yes, Loooord.
Yes, Holy Spirit.
My heart is an altar and your love is the flame. My heart is an altar and your love is the flame. Nazirite Spirit, possess me. John the Baptist, Possess me. Burn. Yes, Lord.

The preacher calls us to the altar. I stand, feeling powerful, feeling sure. Energy surges through my legs as I make my way forward. I'm standing in a row with a hundred other teens. I'm not alone. These are my people. We are the people who will be in the history books. We are the people who will see signs and wonders. We will see God.

I want to be a Nazirite.

The preacher is slowly making his way across the altar, sprinkling anointing oil on the feet of each new consecrated teenager. We are singing a song about burning for God, and I feel the words bubbling over from my soul. A flame flickers deep inside me, and as I sing, I feel it spreading all over my body.

I feel a warm touch on my shoulder. It's the preacher. He takes a whiff of air near my scalp and closes his eyes.

"Oooh, the Spirit is doing something sweet in this one. Whoa, I feel it. Whew!" And he breaks out into laughter.

The Spirit is doing something sweet indeed.

My heart is an altar and your love is the flame.

The anointing oil seeps into the canvas of my shoes, leaving dark stains near the big toe of the new red Vans I picked out for my sixteenth birthday two weeks ago.

"God won't give you your heavenly language if you don't move your mouth. Start speaking, move your jaw, let words fall out, any words at all," the preacher shouts. Thirty-six hours ago, speaking in tongues still freaked me out, and now I'm a Nazirite and I'm asking God to fill me with a heavenly language on the last night of this retreat.

"Yes Jesus, yes Jesus, yes Jesus," I say over and over, loosening my jaw and giving the Holy Spirit the chance to enter. I wish I could come up with something deep to say, closer to how Jessa prays, in lyrical metaphors and beautiful petitions based on obscure passages in the Old Testament. But I guess I could be worse. One guy near me is shouting "Watermelon!" again and again to receive his spiritual language.

"Yes Jesus, yes Jesus, yes Jesus." The words stop sounding like themselves, but I keep going. A warm sensation grows in my chest and works its way down my spine like a slow wave.

Yes-Jesus-yes-Jesus-thank-you-God-thank-you-God-thank-you-God-thank-you-God-yes-Jesus. My heart flutters, in a good way, and tears flow. *Yes-Jesus-yes-Jesus.* I clumsily stretch my arms higher. I get a picture of Jesus's robe dangling inches above me, and feel if I just reached a few inches higher I could feel the garment of God. People at church talk about having visions from the Lord, and this is my first yet.

Yes-Jesus-thank-you-God.

"Keep talking, get your mouth moving. Any words will do! Holy Spirit, fill this place with your power," the preacher says, thrusting from his hips. His voice is as sandpapery as ever. Behind him, the worship band plays a song about Jesus fulfilling all our hopes and dreams. I keep babbling, exhilarated and terrified at the thought of finally receiving the gift for myself. I remember the first time I saw speaking in tongues at that summer camp. It was so scary then, and it's still a little scary now. But the preacher says tongues are a physical evidence of a true life for God. I want the evidence.

I feel something cold and sharp scraping the back of my neck. I whip around to see a heavyset middle-aged woman with crimson lipstick and long red fingernails pulling me in for a hug.

"The Lord told me he has something special for you tonight," the woman says. "Do you mind if I pray for you?"

She places one hand on my forehead and another on the small of my back. Her touch titillates me, not in the same way I imagine it would if a boy were to touch me there, I don't think, but in an enchanted spiritual way. I close my eyes and take a deep breath of the thick Holy Spirit air permeating the altar.

"Rigantee-mee-yaw," she says and exhales a big dramatic breath like Jane Fonda does on Mom's workout videos. I peek up and see her waving her hands over me in a sweeping fluid motion like a witch crooning over her potions. I shut my eyes.

This voice pops up inside. *This stuff is all made up, you know.*

I fight the thought with my whole body. *No, no. It can't be. Jesus, I need to believe this is real. This is real. This is real. Jesus. This is real.* I realize I am saying this out loud. The prayer woman coos in agreement.

"This is real!" I shout.

"Claim it!" the prayer woman says.

My throat tightens and my tongue swells up and quivers on the roof of my mouth, and my lungs feel like they are on fire. A warm, tingly feeling spreads through my body. My jaw begins to rattle, and my tongue curls up and freezes, as if it is held hostage by an outside force.

Overcome, I open my mouth.

Words I have never heard before pour out from my lips as my tongue dances around my teeth, making a long string of *Z* sounds and clipped vowels in rapid fire syllables. I feel bile rising in my throat. I don't recognize my own voice. It sounds so melodious, so unlike the harsh, stammering voice I know as my own.

"Hallelujah! Hallelujah!" the prayer woman shouts.

I begin sobbing as the words flow. My tongue is generous in its crafting of syllable after elegant syllable without my consent, and it sounds so exotic and beautiful. Never in my life have I used so many *Z* sounds. With each one, my teeth and throat vibrate.

I don't think I can stop, even if I want to.

The prayer woman is celebrating my victory in the Spirit. She kicks off her leather sandals and dances around me. "Oh, the Spirit is strong in this one. Breakthrough, Jesus! Shakotinga-linga!" she cries.

I feel like I am soaring with Jesus. The preacher was right when he said the Holy Spirit is better than any pleasure the world offers. I want to bask in this moment forever.

This is real.

The preacher is still on stage, yelling prayers about sacrificing our lives to Jesus. I flap my arms in the air and clap my hands. The words keep flowing like a volcano, moving and growing inside and erupting at the tip of my tongue. I put my fingers to my hot cheeks. Although I can't see my face, I imagine it golden and glowing with the Spirit of God.

"Heaven is groaning right now for you! Moaning from the heavens!" The prayer woman hugs me tight and puts her hands on my hips. She feels soft and warm and radiant, like a Spirit-filled Pillsbury Doughboy. We sway together. She is whispering in my ear and speaking truth over my life. I continue to speak in tongues, stopping only to take breaths. My legs grow weak, and I feel my body's weight moving back and forth from my heels to my toes, more exaggerated with each sway. I know I am losing my balance, but I don't mind. I am safe in the arms of the prayer woman.

My legs go numb; the prayer lady begins swaying into me with more pressure, and then lets me fall backwards. Two other women standing behind me catch me inches before I hit the floor. They lay me down gently on my back, and I can hear them muttering in tongues over me.

I shout my new language from the floor. The prayer woman kisses me on my forehead and walks away, leaving a ring of warm, pasty saliva on my skin. I'm beat, so I close my eyes and let the prayers of one hundred worshipping teens lull me into a deep sleep.

When I awaken, I have no sense for how much time has passed. My muscles are warm and relaxed, my heart worn out and peaceful. I pull myself up with spongy arms and legs and sit on the floor. Something miraculous happened, I remember that much.

I look around the room for the woman who prayed for me. My friends from youth group as well as groups of teens from other churches are scattered and huddled on the floor of the altar. The ceiling lights have been turned on and the worship band is gone; instead, soft music plays from the church sound system. The preacher is nowhere to be seen. Dahlia and Heather are hugging and wiping their tears. Jessa sits cross-legged on the floor, scribbling in her journal. My brother and the other boys are in their seats. They are not talking or touching, and they have somber looks on their faces. One of our youth group parent volunteers is tickling her teenage son's back as he sleeps on her shoulder.

On the drive home, I feel high. I've never tried drugs, but this is how I imagine them to feel. I'm sipping my strawberry shake from In-n-Out Burger, my mind soaring and every hair on my body standing up. My baptism into the Holy Spirit is like the start of a whole new life. The old Carly was worldly and full of sin, but the new Carly is heavenly and full of the Spirit. This is the night everything changed. I will call it year 0 AB, After Baptism.

One of the boys from youth group, Brady, initiates a game of backseat Rock-Paper-Scissors. We get really into the game, and I catch myself giggling a lot. Brady is kind of cute; I wonder what it would be like to kiss him. I'm surprised by my own thought. I kind of thought the new Carly wouldn't think such lustful things, that my mind would be too preoccupied by the Spirit to be distracted by such trivia.

First sin, after baptism.

Brady and I simultaneously shout, "You cheated!"

"Jinx!" I say.

"Jinx?" Jessa says from the driver's seat, making that raised-eyebrow face, the same one she made when she caught me and the other girls singing the secular song on the way to camp. "What do you think a jinx is, Carly?"

"Oh," I say. I have been playing the *jinx* game since Jane taught me when I was seven years old. I never thought about its meaning. The rules are if you and someone else say the same thing in unison, the first person to shout, "jinx" makes the other person stay quiet until you release them from your spell. "I guess technically a jinx is a spell you cast on someone."

"That's right," Jessa says. "We don't cast spells on each other."

Casting a spell on someone. I guess that makes my second sin after baptism.

I think Jessa is being a little uptight. It's just a kid's game.

Third sin.

I chastise myself for thinking that way. After all, the Nazirite preacher said even the tiniest sins can neuter our heart for God, so I suppose saying "jinx" could distract us from our calling. I should admire Jessa's conviction.

Two hours ago, I was on the floor, drinking in the Holy Spirit for the first time. And now, here I am, already back to my old ways, sinning three times on the drive home. I thought the Holy Spirit was supposed to change everything. I whisper the prayer I cried at the altar. *God, break me off from the Spirit of this world. My heart is an altar, and your love is the flame.*

Pastor Frank calls the youth group to the front of the church during his sermon the next morning. I make my way forward with my Nazirite friends, feeling bold and strong.

"You guys aren't just any youth group, I can see it on your hearts," he says, looking at us, but speaking to the congregation. He is an hour into his sermon, and it's all been about us, the Voice in the Desert Youth, how godly and powerful we all are. "You are a special people of God. You have embraced the Spirit, and God is moving among you. Praise the Lord!"

Of course we are special, I think. We are going to make history together. I look to my left and see Dahlia, a huge smile on her face. Last night, God gave her a word over her life. God told her she was supposed to dig deeper into the Spirit and not just take her parents' faith as her own. God said he would make her dreams of being a famous singer and actress come true if she obeyed.

"The Spirit came down on our youth this weekend! Anyone who wants more of God, come down to the altar right now and have the youth group pray for you," Pastor Frank says.

I've only had the Spirit for twelve hours, and now I'm supposed to pour it on someone else, and I no longer feel bold and strong. I feel unqualified. But fifteen adult churchgoers are walking in my direction and I have to do something. I can't back down; I am a Nazirite. I wonder if I should tickle people's necks and dance like the prayer woman did for me last night. Cindy hops to the piano bench and begins playing. The music helps me relax.

I place my hand on a woman's shoulder. Her name is Kathy and she has two young kids, but that's about all I know about her. I will have to keep my prayers vague.

"Jesus, just bless Kathy. Holy Spirit, fill her," I pray, stroking her back.

"Yes Lord!" she whispers, lifting her flappy arms in the air.

"Holy Spirit, take her to deep places," I say. That was a line I heard someone at the altar say last night. I think it sounds pretty good.

"Yes, Lord!" she moans. I guess my prayers are working, so I keep going.

I switch to my new prayer language with all the *Z*'s. I sound like a gazelle jumping in the meadow, so melodic and perfect and bubbling with beautiful tone, although doesn't feel quite as euphoric as the first time. No bile rises in my throat, and no visions of Jesus come to mind. I am aware and in control of my body.

Kathy, on the other hand, is losing control. She is shaking. I'm not sure if she's having a seizure, or if I did something wrong or what. But I think I've seen enough altar calls now to know this is supposed to happen. Her face twists in pain, and tears are running down her neck. Her voice is unrecognizable, all choppy and wheezy. I want to make her feel better, to stop whatever is happening to her. This is worse than just regular altar call shaking. Plus, her face is so tortured, like the girl from *The Exorcist* (which I have only seen posters for), and it frightens me. I need to help her calm down.

"Fill Kathy with peace," I pray and rest my hand on her quaking shoulder. The shaking subsides a little. "Yes, just fill her with your peace, Holy Spirit," I say.

Pastor Frank and Jacob come alongside me. They listen to my prayers for peace and then they join in with their own prayers.

"Holy Spirit, break Kathy in this moment," Jacob shouts.

"Peace," I say, in a pathetic little voice.

"Spirit of Jehovah, consume Kathy with the fire of your presence," Frank prays. His voice is ten times louder than mine.

"Peace," I say.

"Break her!" Jacob shouts.

"Peace," I say.

"Consume her!" Frank shouts.

"Peace," I say.

Kathy collapses to her knees and shrieks like a wild animal. *Peace, God. Please give her peace.*

She's lurching around kicking on the floor when from her mouth comes a screeching noise like a hawk being shot in the air.

"Yes, Lord!" Jacob says.

I step back and watch Kathy curl under Pastor Frank and Jacob's prayers. *Kathy doesn't want peace*, I think. Kathy wants to burn under the fire of the Holy Spirit. I am an idiot for praying the wrong thing. I gulp. I can do this.

"God, just break Kathy," I say.

"Yes, Lord, break Kathy!" Jacob says.

"Yes!" Pastor Frank says.

Kathy utters a cutting primal scream and falls on her face.

"Yes! Yes!"

She's on the floor, panting and screaming and jolting up and down like she's being struck with lightning.

"Break her!" I say. Her heavy panting begins to slow, and her breathing grows longer and deeper.

"Yes," Pastor Frank says, his voice quieting.

Kathy's convulsing ebbs to an occasional twitch. Her eyes are closed, and her tears are dried on her face. She looks peaceful. I look at Jacob, who flashes me a smile that says *good job*. I beam. I think I am beginning to understand. The Holy Spirit needed to break Kathy before she could have peace. Peace would come, but not until after the fire.

The other adults at the altar had met the fire as well, and everyone is quiet now. Cindy is still playing pretty piano music, and Dahlia leans in to give me a long hug. I look down at Kathy, who is so blissful on the floor.

A wave of pride overcomes me. I helped someone meet the Spirit. I gloat in the control I had over Kathy as I prayed, that I could pray for her to be broken and she would writhe under my hands. Maybe this is what they mean when they talk about the *power* of the Holy Spirit.

After church, Jessa comes up to me and puts her arm around me. "Want to hang out today, chica? I want to get to know you better," she says. "How about the mall?"

I'm still feeling floaty and spiritual from the night before, and now from this morning, and I am so tired my neck feels like it can't hold up my head. But I agree to go. I don't want to miss out on spending time with Jessa. This is the first time she's noticed me. Plus, I am still on a cloud of my spiritual high. Going home, back to my regular life with chores and distractions, might strip away the magic. I know it can't last forever, but I want it to last one more day.

"Sounds super fun. Can Dahlia come too?" I ask.

"Sure. Girl time!"

Before we can leave for girl time, Jessa says she needs to pray with Jacob and her mom, Cindy, to debrief from the weekend. Dahlia and I wait outside, leaning against a concrete ledge with other kids from youth group. People begin to disperse, going about their Sundays. Some of the guys are off to the movies, others have family obligations. We have plans with Jessa, we tell them all.

Pretty soon it's just the two of us waiting, and no Jessa in sight, although we can hear her. Someone is playing an old hymn on the piano inside the church and three voices blend in harmony. Their noises are muffled, but I can tell Jacob, Jessa, and Cindy are wailing and praying in tongues.

"How much longer do you think they'll be?" I ask Dahlia. She shrugs.

"You just never know," she says. I wonder if I detected a hint of irritation in her tone.

I am satiated on the God front after everything that happened at the conference. I wonder how Jacob and Jessa can want—or even have the capacity for—yet another deep spiritual epiphany? Don't they ever get tired?

"I guess you can never spend too much time with God," I say.

"I guess so," Dahlia says.

Dahlia and I lie on the concrete and are on the brink of falling asleep when Jessa comes out. The sun is hanging lower in the sky than before we dozed. She has dark circles under her eyes. She kisses Jacob goodbye, and half-apologizes for making us wait. She says they didn't expect the Spirit to move like that. The way she talks about the Spirit makes it sound like it's not something humans can control. I think I'm starting to get it.

We wander the mall aimlessly, Jessa, Dahlia, and I. I take in the hum of chatting shoppers, the harsh fluorescent lighting, and the fruity smell from the food court Jamba Juice. It all has new meaning now. I am not just a homeschooled girl in a mall; I'm not here to shop. I mean, I am, but it's bigger than that. I have a purpose.

I'm the hands and feet of Jesus.

A pack of teenagers with piercings and spiky hair passes us. With my new spiritual eyes, I no longer see them as peers too cool for me. They are souls who need my intercession. It no longer matters if they see me as a nerd, or don't see me at all. I have something they want, something they need. When we walk by Victoria's Secret, I avert my eyes from the black-and-white posters of busty women in push-up bras. Victoria's Secret is no longer a store where girls prettier than me buy expensive underwear. It is one of the devil's strongholds, and my job is to pray against it. God is counting on me.

"It's like my eyes have been opened to a whole new world," I tell Dahlia, squeezing a gob of cucumber melon lotion from the tester bottle at Bath & Body Works. Jessa is on the other side of the store, sniffing the candles. "I see what I was missing all this time."

"Aw, I'm so happy for you. Now we can share this together," Dahlia says. "Here, smell this one."

"Oh that one's nice. What is it?"

"Sweet Pea. I think I'm going to get it," she says.

We don't say much after this. We don't need to. We are resting in the unspoken bond of two people brought together by a force bigger than ourselves.

After we eat heaping plates of orange chicken at Panda Express, Jessa says she wants to buy a new swimsuit, so we head to Macy's and watch her try on dozens. Dahlia yawns and sits cross-legged on the fitting room floor while I struggle to keep my eyes open, but each time Jessa emerges in a new swimsuit, we smile and rave about it.

She finally picks out a pale yellow tankini with a price tag of just under one hundred dollars. She can't decide if she should spend so much on a swimsuit, and I tell her she should get it if she feels good in it, even though I only buy my swim attire at Target. I mostly just want her to be done with trying them on today because I've reached the point of exhaustion.

"Jacob will think it's a lot of money, but he'll be so attracted to my body in it," Jessa says. I blush, but I'm secretly hoping I too will have a husband someday who finds me attractive in a bathing suit.

"Well then, definitely get it. Look good for your husband!" Dahlia says.

Jessa buys the swimsuit and keeps the receipt. She says she will try it on for Jacob and let him decide if she should keep it.

On the forty-minute drive back to Pine Canyon in Jessa's car, we sing along to a worship CD playing from the stereo. I close my eyes and lean my head against the backseat window, wiped out but elated for this new life—both as a Nazirite and in my new church. I have friends now. A group. And we have a purpose. A calling. A reason for it all.

"I sense the Lord is doing something very special between us," Jessa says. "I'm so thankful that you two are my girls."

My girls. I like the way that sounds.

Five

Jessa Rowan has been a pastor's daughter most of her life, ever since Pastor Frank quit the printing business for ministry. The middle of three daughters, Jessa is known as the most spiritual one. Her older sister is independent and loud, a college graduate into conservative politics, and her younger sister is into fashion and tennis. Jessa isn't really into *anything* except Jesus, and everyone knows she has something special.

Jessa seems to take to godliness naturally, unlike me, the person who is always fighting temptations and dwelling on unspiritual thoughts. Jessa has an advantage because being godly is all she's ever known. Her whole childhood revolved around church and her devout Christian family, and she didn't move out until she got married.

She doesn't know much about current events or the world outside church, and sometimes I find myself annoyed by this. I mean, there's a lot of stuff I don't know too, but Jessa has never even heard of the movie *Grease*. I want to tease her for what she doesn't know, but I can't. She has this confidence—a pride even—in who she is, and I can't help but be in awe of her. It's something in the way she talks in definitive statements, as if her existence alone is enough to give her authority, or the way she holds her tall frame, her feet planted in the ground and her neck held high. She is Jessa, and she is loved. By God, by her parents, by Jacob, by me. And she is wise in the important things. She knows the Bible inside and out, and she is a committed Prayer Warrior.

I want to be just like her.

At the age of twenty-one, she married Jacob in her parents' backyard, where Jacob surprised her with a song he had written about their sacred love. Jessa wore a modest white satin gown with sleeves and a high neckline. Pastor Frank led the ceremony. Later, their guests played badminton into the sunset as Jacob and Jessa snuck behind a barn to kiss. During sparkling cider toasts, Jacob took the microphone and announced that God spoke to him and Jessa and told them to name their relationship "Three Cords," based on a verse in Ecclesiastes that says a strand of three is not easily broken. Each of them represented a cord, and Jesus was the third cord. Their friends and family wept with them. I wasn't there, but Jessa loves to show pictures and retell the stories, so I feel like I was.

The youth minister position at Pine Canyon Assemblies of God is part-time, and I'm not sure how Jessa and Jacob got the job. I don't think Pastor Frank *interviewed* them or anything. However much money they make from the church, it must not be enough to pay the bills, because Jacob works early mornings at UPS, and Jessa fixes coffee drinks part-time at the Starbucks a few towns over. They live in a small, newly constructed buttercream-yellow house on the outskirts of town, a few yards from the interstate. Their backyard, which they dream of someday landscaping, is all red dirt and exposed roots. There isn't a room in the house where the frantic hiss of cars and cargo trucks can't be heard. But they don't care. They are so happy, and their house is cozy and homey with colorful woven rugs and art prints that say BLESS OUR HOME.

I spend as many afternoons as I can with Jessa in her little yellow house. She enjoys the company, as Jacob works many more hours than she does, and I love learning about life from her.

"This is Jacob's favorite dish I make," Jessa proudly says one afternoon I'm at her house. She has a slight lisp from the clear braces she recently got. "It's chicken Alfredo." She flicks a pack of powdered ranch dressing mix three times, dumps it into a pot of boiling milk and diced chicken, and stirs.

"I used to use Hidden Valley Ranch, but would you believe that the generic brand from WinCo tastes better?" Jessa says. "Cooking is all about experimenting like that."

She scoops a ladle of the pasta and white sauce into a bowl and hands it to me. I blow on a forkful of noodles and white sauce and take a bite. It's so salty I can barely swallow.

"It's great," I say.

"Jacob loves when I cook for him," she says. "I love doing things for him that make him happy."

They want children someday, she tells me—two boys and a girl. Jacob is hoping to get a dog, a German shepherd or a chocolate Labrador. They spend their weekends sleeping in, reading the Bible together, praying and cuddling, going to the movies or the park. I inhale her stories. Jacob and Jessa are so passionately in love. They are the people God gave to each other. They have found the one and only person God chose for them in the world, and they are going to spend the rest of their lives under God's perfect plan.

"I want to make my husband happy someday too," I say.

"Yeah? And what kind of husband do you dream of?" she asks. She is wolfing down her pasta while mine gets cold.

"Someone godly and strong who can lead me into the things of the Lord," I say.

"God wants to give that to you, Carly," she says. I'm jealous of her certainty in God's good plans.

"I hope so," I say.

"You know, you are going to be a mighty force for the Lord," she says, clearing our Alfredo bowls. She lights a vanilla candle on the kitchen counter between us. "I see it in you."

"God has been revealing that to me lately, too," I say. "I'm not sure in what way yet—maybe I'll be a missionary, or a youth pastor like you."

It doesn't sound like my voice coming out—I always used to say I wanted to be a writer and a homesteader with cows and chickens roaming around me. But it seems like all the godliest people are called to ministry. I am godly, or at least trying to be, so I am probably called to ministry too.

"How have your quiet times been lately? What have you been praying for?" she asks.

At that moment, Jacob comes through the front door, sweaty in his tight brown uniform. His eyes are dull and he doesn't bounce from his feet like he does at youth group. He has been loading packages into a delivery truck since 4 a.m., Jessa explains.

"Did you make Alfredo today? I can smell it," he says.

"Yep, honey. I made it for Carly," she says.

"Oh, that's nice," he says. The muscles on his face are droopy.

"Don't worry, there is some left for you. When you wake up," she says. He kisses Jessa on the mouth and shuffles off to the bedroom to take a nap.

I get up to leave, and Jessa tells me I should stay. But I know it is time to go. With Jacob home, his favorite dish on the stove, and a vanilla candle burning on the counter, I feel like an awkward, dangling Fourth Cord. I soon learn Jacob's schedule and work around it, maximizing my times alone with Jessa. Without Jacob around, I feel like Jessa and I have a special intimacy, a kind of closeness that I haven't experienced with anyone before. We have a connection that she doesn't have with the other girls from youth group, and that makes me feel prized.

Most of the time, that is. Sometimes Jessa's stances—especially the ones on modesty—scare me a little. She doesn't seem like herself when she talks about modesty. Her voice gets lower and she talks in whole phrases that sound copied from books she's read. I'm thinking about this on the night she holds a special lesson in modesty for the Missionettes.

"Again, girls, it's not about rules, it's about honoring the Spirit," Jessa says, putting a hand on her heart.

Dahlia crosses her arms and sighs.

"Look, if I wear anything but a loose T-shirt, I show cleavage. It's not fair because I'm not trying to look sexy, but I always get the signals from Pastor Cindy," Dahlia says. I drop my jaw in Dahlia's direction and give her an inward high five. She's saying exactly what's on my mind. Last week, Cindy made eye contact with me in the middle of a special youth group Bible study, her cat-like blue eyes ablaze. I grinned back at her, thinking she was being impacted by the message, and she turned her lips in a prim smile. Then she placed her hand on her chest and tapped three times. I looked down at my chest. Sure enough, my shirt had crept down again. I pulled at the fabric around my breasts and sat up straight. Cindy nodded, and turned her attention back to Jacob's lesson without even flinching. I tried to focus on the lesson, hoping nobody noticed my bright red face. This is the sign language Cindy uses to tell us girls when we are showing too much skin without embarrassing us, or at least embarrassing us less than if she brought it up in front of everyone. One tap on her chest means our shirt is too low. Three taps mean it's *really* low. A tug at the bottom hem of her shirt means our shirt is too short. A pat on her thighs means we should cross our legs. With a smooth, wordless flick of her hand, Cindy sends us away to cover up. None of us talks about Cindy's gestures or what they mean because we all know—until Dahlia tonight.

"Well, you know my Mom does that for all of us, including me. She does it to protect our brothers from stumbling. And to answer your question, Dahlia, I believe each of us is responsible for what we have," Jessa says. Even though she is addressing Dahlia, she is looking right at me. Cindy must have told Jessa about my immodesty the other night.

"So basically, the bigger chest we have, the more fabric we have to wear," Dahlia says.

"I know it's hard sometimes," Jessa says. "Trust me, I know. Let me tell you a story."

I have a feeling I know what story she is going to tell, and I shift in my seat. Jessa told it to me before during one of our hangout times at her house, and I thought it was creepy. I settle back into the squishy plaid couch and curl my legs under my hips. The Missionettes recently started meeting in the home of one of the old church ladies instead of the storage closet we used to squeeze into. Even though we meet offsite now, we still attend Pastor Frank's worship portion before caravanning over to Sister Marybeth's house.

"When I was twenty years old, I was just starting to date Jacob," she says. All the girls squeal, the way they always do when Jessa talks about Jacob. I sit quietly, picking at the wrinkly pleather cover of my Bible, trying not to shudder. "I wanted to look pretty for him in new clothes that weren't from the second-hand store," she says. "So my dad took me to Ross Dress for Less to help me pick out some nice

clothes for my new boyfriend. It was such a fun afternoon, and I felt
so special. Girls, I hope you have a daddy who takes you shopping.

"He sat on a little bench in the waiting area while I tried on so
many outfits. My favorite of everything were these bubble-gum-
pink flared jeans. Oh boy, I loved how those jeans felt and looked. I
twirled around the fitting room, admiring how long my legs looked
in them. I knew Jacob would just love these pants. They would go
perfectly with my brown clogs. And they were so comfortable. They
moved with me. They hugged my hips without constricting. And
that's not even the best part—they were on sale for only twelve dollars," she says.

"You got them, right?" one of the newer girls says, lying on her
belly on Sister Marybeth's orange shag carpet, with her chin propped
on her elbows and her feet kicking around like a Disney Princess. She
obviously hasn't heard the story before.

"No," Jessa says.

"What? Why?" the girl asks.

"I burst out of the fitting room to show my dad, and he said,
'Absolutely not.' I was shocked. I whined and asked him why. He told
me to take a few steps toward the full-length mirror, so I did. Then
he asked me if I noticed how the pants make a V-shape in my crotch
when I walk," she says.

I wince, and immediately try to cover it with a smile.

"I looked down, and sure enough, the pants made a V-shape
around the crotch area," she says. "Oh, but I loved them anyway. I
begged Dad, but he stood firm." She says *crotch* in this loud voice,
clamping her tongue down hard on the word's ugly consonant ending.
It sounds like a filthy word coming from her, and I'm disgusted just
thinking what it would sound like coming from Pastor Frank.

"I was so heartbroken that day, and even a little angry. But now, I look back and I'm so thankful that my father took a stand. I cherish the memory and it's been a lesson for me on obeying our spiritual authority even when it doesn't make sense to us, especially when it comes to modesty issues," she says. "It's tough for us girls, especially when we want to look cute and stylish. But I am positive we can look good without compromising."

Dahlia nods like she agrees. I'm trying not to think about Pastor Frank talking about the shape of his daughter's crotch in tight pants. I mean, he's my *pastor*. But then, what do I know about how fathers are supposed to raise godly daughters? I keep quiet and look at my chest to make sure I'm properly covered.

After the lesson, Dahlia and I hide out in my car so we don't have to talk to anyone.

"It's not fair," she says. She sounds angry. "Heather gets to wear whatever she wants, but we have to cover everything."

It's true. The petite girls in youth group get away with wearing the cute frilly tank tops that are so trendy right now. Heather, who is flat chested, even wears *halter tops* in the summer, ones that snugly wrap her torso. But girls like Dahlia and I can't even get away with wearing a scoop-neck shirt without getting the taps from Cindy. It's the whole responsible-for-what-we-have-thing.

"And while we're on the subject . . . A *V*? Seriously, a *V* when she walks? All pants do that," she says.

I laugh hard. This is why Dahlia and I are friends.

"I know. I mean, we're talking about a V-shaped body part here. What other shape is it supposed to make when we walk? A *square*?" I say.

"Was it just me, or were the tiny girls looking kind of smug?" Dahlia says.

"Yay for them and their cute tank tops."

"Well, at least we have boobs," she says.

I laugh. I have never heard Dahlia say the word *boob* before. It sounds rebellious and exciting.

"Amen," I say. "Boobs."

We giggle and toss the word *boob* back and forth, like a secret. Each time we say the word, we say it stronger and with more pride. We aren't supposed to be proud of our bodies like this, but here we are, letting our pride smolder.

I feel guilty about these talks with Dahlia, which after that night, happen more and more frequently. Jessa catches us talking about boobs at In-n-Out a few weeks later, and she gives Dahlia a glare, and me a sad, hurt look. I feel myself splitting my personality for Jessa to approve of me. Around Dahlia, I am sharp, maybe even sassy. Around Jessa, I am innocent and godly. I am a sponge for all the things she has to impart on me. I like both versions of myself, but only one version gets to be best friends with the youth pastor.

I find myself lying under a purple patchwork quilt on Jacob and Jessa's bed, listening to Jessa breathe. The room is flooded with the lights and roars from the interstate. I never thought I would be this close to Jessa Rowan, not in a million years. But when Jacob left town for the night and Jessa asked me to keep her company, I jumped at the chance to have more time alone with her.

"Jacob and I have had some very special times on this bed," she says. It sounds like she is crying. I knew I shouldn't have joined her on this bed—but she said she didn't want to sleep alone. Now I am picturing Jacob and Jessa naked, having "special times" and wishing I were in the guest room instead.

"That's so awesome," I mumble.

She gets quiet again, and I hold my breath. I hope she's done talking. "So many good memories. Sacred memories," she says. My cheeks boil.

"Maybe you should sleep on the other bed after all. I think I need to keep this one just for me and Jacob," she says.

I move to the twin bed in the guest room, grateful to not be on the marriage bed yet hurt that Jessa kicked me out. It's just a bed, after all. There isn't anything sacred about a bed. Or maybe there is. I wouldn't know because I am single and probably will be for life.

I'm drifting off to sleep when I feel something brushing my shoulder. Jessa is hovering over me.

"Can I sleep in here with you?" she asks. "I don't want to be alone."

"Sure," I mumble.

Jessa curls up next to me. On one side, I'm smothered by Jessa, and the other side I'm clinging to the edge of the narrow mattress. Within minutes, she is snoring. Jessa wraps one leg around my hips. Our bodies are hot and sticky pressed up to each other. I'm not used to sharing a bed. I lie flat on my back, wide awake, and pass the hours by until dawn.

Pastor Frank is preaching on the end times again, like he has for the last eight weeks. He's in the middle of his Sunday morning sermon, only it isn't Sunday morning anymore. It is Sunday afternoon.

Sunday services at Pine Canyon Assemblies of God do not cease to bore and confuse me, despite my passion for Jesus. I thought that would change after becoming a Nazirite, but I still find Pastor Frank's sermons hard to follow. And long.

He is pretty sure we are living in the last days and wants to make sure we are all prepared for the rapture, if it should happen in our lifetime, which it probably will. Candace always says she doesn't know when the rapture will happen, but she doesn't think she will die of old age. This end-of-the-world talk always freaks me out. I kind of like the world and would like to live my full life here. Talk of Jesus returning early doesn't comfort me the way it should. I know that makes me unspiritual.

Second Coming of Christ or not, I'm dying for some Chinese food right now. Shrimp with vegetables, the same lunch plate I've ordered at Schezuan Garden since I can remember. With fried rice instead of steamed. Hot and sour soup. A crispy egg roll on the side.

Pastor Frank shouts something about the "Bosom of Abraham." I perk up. The word *bosom* makes me laugh. But this kind of bosom is connected to prophecies in Revelation and the Old Testament, apparently. Not that funny, I guess. Pastor Frank's voice grates on my ears. I won't admit that to anyone, but I just can't get used to his yelling and long-windedness, as much as I respect him as my pastor.

Jessa sits to my left, ferociously writing notes. Everyone takes notes during Pastor Frank's sermons, but his daughters take the most. I think it's kind of funny. It's their *dad*. I guess if my dad had the Spirit of God, I would take notes when he spoke too, but it still seems a little weird. I try to take notes, but Pastor Frank's sermons are hard to follow. His stomping around the pulpit and demonstrative hand motions distract me from his message. And the messages themselves are confusing too. Tangents lead to tangents, and he never seems to follow a sermon series or organized topics. He moves as the Spirit directs him. I love the Spirit, although I do wish it could be a bit tidier. But the Holy Spirit doesn't like to be cut, curbed, or restrained. I am wise enough to know that by now.

I wish I had packed a snack. Oh, a Seven-Layer Burrito from Taco Bell would be so good right now. No sour cream. And a Double

Decker Taco. I can taste the salty, crumbly beef. I can feel its grease running down my wrist.

I peek at the cell phone my parents let me borrow. It is 1:13 p.m.

Pastor Frank rolls out a whiteboard easel from the back storage closet where we used to hold Missionettes. He is inspired to draw a chart of the Bosom of Abraham. He must be talking about hell, because he draws cartoonish orange flames at the bottom of his chart.

One man gets up to leave. Pastor Frank darts his eyes to the back of the room. He *hates* it when people walk out during his sermons. This is a little tricky because some people work on Sunday afternoons. Working on the Sabbath is acceptable because Jesus himself broke Sabbath laws, but Pastor Frank always makes sure people know the very valid reason why someone is leaving in the middle of church, so nobody thinks they are leaving just because they want to.

"Brother Craig has to go to work," Pastor Frank says. Craig looks up, embarrassed. "Bless you, Brother Craig." The entire congregation turns to Craig and waves goodbye.

Most people don't leave church early though. In fact, they keep their enthusiasm up until the very end, shouting "Amen" and clapping, and when it is finally over, they gush on about how powerful it was.

"I want to leave you with this one last thought," Pastor Frank says, after Craig has shut the door. I perk up in my chair. My back is stiff from sitting. Of course, one last thought becomes two last thoughts, which turns into another side-sermon. I check my cell phone again. It is 1:45 p.m.

"I'll let you out of here soon, I promise," Pastor Frank says. "Just one last thought."

The congregation laughs. One old man shouts, "Amen!"

I still don't like the way people encourage Pastor Frank to go on forever. I look around. People don't seem bored. I must be the only one. Sometimes I fantasize about doodling in my notebook, but I would never do something so disrespectful in church. I would be afraid Pastor Frank would call attention to it in front of everyone, the way he does when someone doesn't raise their hands when he asks them to.

"One last thought" morphs into a prayer, a soft one at first, which grows louder and then gives birth to a baby sermon within the prayer. I am lethargic from being so sedentary. My eyelids droop. As a jowl-shaking Pastor Frank shouts his prayer, I drift off in peace.

"Are you okay, Carly? You have been on my heart this week," I hear a voice say.

I startle from my stupor and look up. It is Jessa leaning over me. Pastor Frank is done preaching and the congregation is milling about. I must have finally fallen asleep.

The other thing that confuses me about Pastor Frank's sermons is their heavy bent toward Israeli politics. We sing a lot of songs about Jerusalem, and we pray a lot of prayers for the defeat of Palestine.

On one such Sunday, Pastor Frank is dancing down the rows of chairs holding a miniature blue and white flag with the Star of David in the center. We are in our twentieth chorus of "Shabbat Shalom." For an overweight man in his fifties, Pastor Frank can really bust a move for the Lord. Others are dancing and claiming victory for Israel over Palestine, while they wave around these huge purple and gold flags. "Your pastor has such a heart for Israel," Cindy says from behind the piano. "Let's support him and unleash a mighty pouring of your presence for God's chosen nation right now!"

"Hallelujah," Pastor Frank says, and puts the flag down. "I feel the Spirit moving me to do something today." He walks over to the unused church organ tucked in the corner of the room. Sitting on top of the organ is a bone-yellow animal horn, like that of a ram. It has black spots down one side, and its opening has the girth of a Quaker Oats can.

He picks up the horn and holds it near his face. Next to the horn, Pastor Frank's normally bloated head looks tiny.

"The shofar," Dahlia's mom whispers to herself. "The shofar, the shofar," the whispers rumble through the crowd. People freeze where they are in the aisle and bring their flags to their sides. I lean forward, trying to see what Pastor Frank is up to. He pulls the horn to his lips and blows. His cheeks puff up like a chipmunk as a flat, baritone sound fills the room.

And something else fills the room with it—the smell of septic tank or death. I cover my nose with my shirt.

People cheer. He blows it again. The smell gets worse. I feel nauseated and try to breathe as little as possible.

"Oh, Holy Mount Zion!" Pastor Frank shouts, and blows again. His face was red at first but is now turning purple.

"Shabbat Shalom!" he says and holds the horn up above his head with both hands. Everyone is clapping and cheering but all I can hear is that haunting monotone note ringing in my ears. The whole church seems to be basking in their deep spiritual moment, unbothered by the stench. I get the sense that something meaningful just happened, something I should know about, something that someone with a heart for Israel would understand. The whole ritual makes me uncomfortable, but I try not to question Pastor Frank because he is much closer to God than me.

Jesus, please give me a heart for Israel, I pray, and I mean it.

As much as I love Pine Canyon Assemblies of God, it's no place I'd invite my friends. Between the service length, the speaking in tongues, and all the stuff about Israel, I can't think of one person I know it wouldn't scare off. It's just one of those things you have to be into to understand. I would tell Jane this when she'd ask me about my new church.

Danny, who has a boldness I envy, invites everyone he knows, and has been praying that his unsaved mother would visit our church for months.

One morning, Danny's prayer is answered, and he is ecstatic. During worship, Danny's mother sits politely as the rest of us raise our hands and wave flags around. I keep glancing to the row ahead of me to see if the Spirit has touched her yet, but she seems hardened. I remember feeling that way not too long ago, so I understand. During the second hour of Pastor Frank's sermon, Danny's mom begins digging through her large Coach bag and pulling out a bunch of trash. Is Danny's mom cleaning out her purse? I guess she's not going to get saved today after all. I feel sad for Danny, who I know will be crushed.

"The holiness of God is whole and complete, lacking nothing. He beckons us into his holiness, his wholeness, because that is the character of the Living God," Pastor Frank says.

She sorts through a handful of paper scraps—gum wrappers, receipts, and old grocery shopping lists. She saves one receipt and puts the rest of the junk in a pile in the empty seat next to her. She reaches her hand back in the bag and finds a half-eaten Powerbar.

"God's name *Jehovah* means 'Provider.' God is our provider God, whole and complete, wholeness," Pastor Frank continues. Sometimes the second hour of his sermons unravel into what sounds like a list of free-association words.

Danny's mom eats the remains of the Powerbar, letting the wrapper crinkle loudly, and puts it on top of her trash pile. I am shocked. Nobody acts like this during Pastor Frank's sermons. Doesn't she know she could get in big trouble? She whips out a round hairbrush and runs it through her long blonde hair.

"Wholeness is found in the Lord's presence; without it, we have nothing, no wholeness, holiness," Pastor Frank says.

She rips out a mat of hair from her brush, and adds the hairball to her growing collection of garbage. Danny leans over and whispers something to her. She shakes her head and goes back to her purse. Danny turns away from her. His brow is furrowed and his arms are crossed and he's slouching in his seat.

"Accept the gift of wholeness in your life from the Living God, accept the provision, *Jehovah-jireh*, my provider," Pastor Frank says. It's now the broken-record stage of the sermon.

Danny's mom gets out her leather wallet and begins organizing her credit cards, frequent-shopper cards, business cards, and various IDs. I am nervous for her. I keep waiting for Pastor Frank to stop his sermon to lecture her. I'm so worried about it my stomach hurts. He seems so distracted by this concept of holiness/wholeness that he hasn't noticed it yet. I hope she stops before he catches it. Pastor Frank is so intense when he's upset.

"Let's pray," he says, but Danny's mom doesn't bow her head. She tosses two Tic-Tacs in her mouth and crunches them loudly.

The sermon finally ends and Danny's mom picks up her hairy, sticky pile of trash and dumps it in the wastebasket without shame. Danny herds her to his car and drives away without saying goodbye to anyone. My heart breaks for Danny because I know he was really looking forward to this. I want to be mad at Danny's mom, but I'm not. I think it's kind of cool she doesn't know to be afraid.

We go to Candlestick Park in San Francisco to see the same preacher who made me a Nazirite.

He's on stage, screaming about the Awakening of revival

around the world while a ten-piece band plays behind him. I'm cold. Shivering, miserable cold, even with my hoodie tied tight around my face. I'm supposed to be praying for revival in the nations, and all I want is a space heater.

"God says, 'Every knee will bow and every tongue will confess,'" he says, rocking in his trademark fashion. "Well, let's claim that for the nations today!"

I cheer. "Yes, give us the nations, God! Turn their hearts to you!"

My entire youth group has been fasting all day, as directed by the preacher, to show God we are serious about our prayers. This isn't a lukewarm "Pizza Party" teen conference, we are told—this is a twelve-hour fasting and sacrificial worship event where we will pour out the power of Jesus on our cities and the world!

Jacob is lying prostrate in the grass that is spray-painted with the San Francisco 49ers emblem. He's moaning praises. Jessa waves a purple flag that she brought from home above her head. Danny is jumping up and down, up and down, his red hair flopping above the crowd. He doesn't stop jumping. What a man of God. I'd say I could just eat him up, but at this point I think I'd rather have a sandwich.

"The Lord is telling me there is someone here who is struggling with same-sex attractions!" The preacher says.

Behind me, I hear weeping. I turn around and see a spindly kid with glasses and curly hair, convulsing with each cry.

"In Jesus name, you are healed right now. Right now!" the preacher says. "*Right now!*"

The kid starts dancing and shouting in tongues. I close my eyes and raise my hands and begin to ask for miracles in my own life. I want to be free from sin and be stronger in Christ. I want Jane to get saved and my parents to get serious about God. I claim victory in all these areas, and I throw in some prayers for Israel, because that's what all the good intercessors do. It's hard for me to wrap my mind around praying for big things, for people I don't know and countries I've never been to. My thoughts keep coming back to myself. I watch Danny lost in prayer. He's swaying and totally basking in the presence of God. I wish I could stay focused on God the way he does.

The sun is lowering behind the metal bleachers in the stadium, and a wind is picking up, blowing chilly air from the bay. The air cuts through my sweatshirt. I rub my ears to keep them warm. They feel stiff. I keep trying to pray, but I can't focus. I've been here for hours, and I'm cold and hungry and all prayed out. I look around and notice most of my youth group has left the field. It's just me, Jacob, Jessa, Danny, Kevin, and a bunch of people I don't know. The preacher is begging for the release of the Spirit of lust in our generation.

I can't give up now. There are still hours left to the day. I raise one hand and try to pray against lust, but I can't concentrate. Leaving the field is what a lukewarm Christian would do, and I especially don't want to look lukewarm in front of Danny.

A shiver runs through my body, and I can't stop my teeth from chattering. I can't handle this anymore. I back away on my toes, and Danny doesn't notice me leaving, thankfully. He's too immersed in his intercession to notice anything else.

I find Dahlia and a few of the guys on the bleachers, perching their feet up on the seats in front of them. They had lost interest in the intercession long before me, they say. *We're supposed to be Nazirites*, I want to lecture them. But who am I to talk? I'm here with them.

We roam around Candlestick Park together with our hands shoved in our pockets, tuning out the cries of people praying for the nations. In the parking lot, we find a youth group eating from paper bags with the yellow Carl's Jr. star. I can smell the grease of their thick beef patties from here. They cluster around a white van with the words HONK IF YOUR BODY IS A LIVING SACRIFICE written in poster paint on the windows. A middle-aged guy with a goatee and bags under his eyes chomps into his Six-Dollar Burger darting his head around in guilt.

Cheaters, we scoff. How lukewarm.

"We gotta get away from that smell," I say. "It's too tempting."

Later, the guys find a pack of cute fourteen-year-old girls to follow around, so Dahlia and I are left to sit in the bleachers by ourselves. We watch the holy movement below us without saying much. I am proud of my passion to do big things and pray for big things, but sometimes I wonder what it would be like to be small, to just eat cheeseburgers and drink Diet Coke and not worry about interceding for the nations. I think of this as we huddle together to stay warm, the hours creeping by in slow motion, our butts frozen from the steel benches we sit on.

Six

I spend the next three months scooping ice cream to save for this trip. I've read and re-read the entry for Romania in Dad's 1964 *R* volume of the encyclopedia. I've prayed for the Lord to prepare the hearts of the lost. I've been counting down the months, and then the days, and now I'm counting down the hours. This will be an adventure of a lifetime—an adventure in spreading the Gospel to the ends of the earth. We will be there for an entire month.

"What's the food like there?" Jane asks. She's lounging on my bed as I'm packing my suitcase. I have my rose lamp on, which emits a soft pink glow over us.

"I hear there's this thing called head-cheese. It's like gelatin and pork fat all mixed together," I say.

"Wow. Take a picture of that for me," she says.

Jane is wearing a low-cut shirt and workout pants. The shirt is tight and white (Jane loves to wear white; it shows off her bronze skin), and I can see the tops of her breasts. I try to go about packing and chatting like nothing is wrong, but I can't stop thinking about how immodest she is right now. I hear a voice whisper in my ear. It's this quiet, persistent voice I hear from time to time now, ever since I was baptized in the Holy Spirit. *Talk to Jane about her shirt*, the voice says.

I can't do that, I tell myself. *I'll hurt her feelings.*

You have to do it for Me, the voice responds. The voice must be God, I think. God is asking me to confront Jane about her immodest shirt. *But God, what would that accomplish?* I ask. *Leave that to Me,* God says. *You are to be a witness for me at all times. Will you obey?*

This might be a test. The preacher and Jacob talk about this—that God will test us to see if we are faithful in the little things before he shows us signs and wonders. I take a deep breath and get ready to confront my friend.

"You're showing a lot of cleavage," I blurt.

"Excuse me?" Jane says.

"I just, um . . . I don't want to do anything that hurts God's heart," I say, stammering. I don't really know what to say. I didn't think about the outcome of this conversation. God told me not to. "Our sin—even what we choose to wear—can block the Holy Spirit from doing amazing things in our lives. Anything we do that isn't godly can hinder it. I don't want to be blamed for blocking the Holy Spirit, do you?"

There. I spat it out. I feel proud of my witness. I obeyed the voice of God. I wait for the heavens to shake.

"Whatever, Carly, you're acting weird. I like to dress comfortable," Jane says.

"I get that," I say. All the fist-pumping talk about burning the hearts of the rebellious now feels fuzzy and distant when I'm hanging out with my old friend.

"Hey have you heard Usher's new album? It's out of control." I haven't heard the new Usher album; in fact, I haven't listened to any secular music at all since I became a Nazirite.

"No," I say.

Jane picks up a shapeless brown T-shirt from the floor, one that I had picked up at K-Mart last week for my trip. The mission organization said to pack loose-fitting, modest clothes only.

"Is this how you're going to dress now?" she asks, throwing the shirt at me. I nod.

"I'm trying to dress more modest for God," I say. Maybe this is how it feels to be persecuted for my faith.

"How are you going to work on your tan this summer in shirts like that?" she asks.

"I'm not thinking about my tan anymore," I say.

Here I am changing the world, and Jane is worried about tan lines. Jane has plans to spend her summer lying out on granite boulders in a swimsuit at the river, like we do every summer. But those kinds of carefree summers are for teenagers who don't have the Fire of God. I can go swimming now and then, but I have more important things demanding my attention this summer. After I return from my trip to Romania, I'll be busy with a bunch of evangelistic outreaches in downtown Pine Canyon, and other youth group events.

I wonder if I am losing Jane. She's always been my best friend—but if we don't have God in common, then what do we really share?

Jane sighs and puts her feet on my wall. I look at her and I realize for the first time that she is beautiful. This hits me like a volleyball to the gut. I guess because I've known her since before I could walk, I never thought about it before. I definitely don't feel self-conscious around her the way I do around other beautiful girls. But now that I've seen it, I'll never un-see it: Jane is striking. I study her in awe. She has straight coffee-bean-colored hair to her mid-back, brown skin with hazel eyes, and a smile that puffs out her cheeks, each of which is covered with exactly seven freckles. For some reason, I am struck with this above everything else. She has the perfect amount of freckles. Now that I think about it, Jane always has a lot of boys at school who want to date her. She usually is too busy playing varsity volleyball to date them, but the point is that she *could* if she wanted to.

Our lives are so different.

Jane and I had different interests from the beginning; she showed athletic promise at a young age, while I took to drama, music, and art. But now that my whole world has become about pursuing Jesus, there is a new canyon between Jane and me, and I worry we will never bridge it. I am hit with desperation for my dear friend to know Jesus the way I do.

"Earth to Carly! Earth to Carly!" Jane says, throwing a pillow at me. "What's on your mind? You're so quiet today."

"Oh, nothing. Hey, you were telling me about that boy from school. What's his name again?"

"Chaz. We should all hang out sometime," she says.

"Yeah, we should, when I get back," I say.

But I'm thinking it won't happen. Tomorrow I'll board a plane to Texas, where I'll be trained for a few days before boarding another plane to Romania. I feel like I'm leaving Jane behind forever.

The dark-skinned man has a layer of skin where his eyes should be. He also has stringy hair with yellow flakes falling out, and a dirty unbuttoned white shirt. His home is made of cardboard, and his kitchen is a fire pit. The least we can do is heal his eyes.

Earlier today, we pulled up in a charter bus to this encampment of poor, nomadic people that morning to perform our evangelistic drama and see what else Jesus might do through us. We are halfway through our month-long trip, and we haven't seen a healing yet. We are all getting antsy for an exciting miracle story to take home to our churches and friends.

Every morning since arriving here in Romania, I curl up on the concrete basketball court to read my Bible and pray. Every morning I read the same passage, the part in Isaiah where God asks, "Who will go for me?" And Isaiah says, "Here am I; send me." I write these words on my wrist in blue ink and carry them with me all day.

Every morning in Romania, after our quiet times, we gather in a dusty field outside our dormitory and sing a cappella, a song about how God will give us the nations if we cry out to him. Our voices rise to God as our ankles rub against thistle weed. Tears roll down my cheek; I've never heard anything quite this beautiful. Every morning, we pray together before we depart for our day of ministry. We tell each other God is going to use us to do something Big. This might be our chance. We circle around the man with no eyes, and I look at the ink on my wrist. *Here am I; send me.*

"Jesus, by your blood, just heal this man right now, realign his cells so that he can see," our leader Caleb prays.

I peek to see if the man's face has grown eyes yet.

"God, you say in your word that if we ask anything in your name, you will grant it. So we just ask that you give this man a pair of eyes that he may be healed, in your name," another kid from our group cries out.

I peek again. *Lord, I believe. Help my unbelief.*

"Lord, just use this miracle as a testimony to your name, that the other people in this encampment would see your mighty work and be saved," I pipe in. I always like to remind God that our requests will benefit him in the long run. The man still has skin over his eye sockets. We continue to pray. "Jesus, just heal this man. Lord, we have the faith of a mustard seed. God, you said that we would do greater things in your name than your own son. Jesus, Jesus, Jesus."

Caleb interrupts.

"Maybe there is someone among us who doubts. One person's doubt could thwart the whole thing. Remember, if we want to see healings, we all have to truly believe God can do it," he says.

We go back into our prayers, upping the level of fervency.

"Lord! Hear our prayers!"

I am the doubter, I realize.

"You said we would do greater things in your name."

I am the reason this poor guy won't be healed.

"Please, Lord. Please."

Lord, help my unbelief.

After we pray for forty-five minutes, Caleb stops us. He warns us that we shouldn't beg God. The man with no eyes staggers away, back to his cardboard house, leaving us crushed.

"We don't know what will happen later. He could still get healed. Maybe he will wake up tomorrow with new eyes. We'll never know," Caleb says. We nod, each of us interpreting what just happened in a way that made sense to us, in a way that still allowed us to believe. I don't think he'll wake up tomorrow with new eyes.

In front of one of the scrap-wood and cardboard shacks to our right, a group of women is listening to music on a battery-powered radio and dancing around together as they wash clothes in a plastic kiddie swimming pool. My new friend Eleanor and I watch them work from a distance.

"They seem so happy," I say.

They see us watching, and stick out their long index fingers, motioning for us to join them.

We look at each other, and look around to see if Caleb is around. He is busy talking to his co-leader, Taylor. We know dancing is against the rules . . . But it looks so fun.

They welcome us with hugs, these women in cotton wrap

dresses and gold teeth. We dance with them to a static-fuzz Romanian pop song. We thrust our hips around with them and throw our arms in the air. We show them the "shopping cart" dance move, and they are roaring with laughter, probably both with us and at us. We don't care. This is the most fun we've had since being here.

Caleb blows his whistle. "Knock it off!" he shouts in our direction. "We gotta go anyway. Say goodbye now." Our dance partners hug us goodbye, and point at us with big hand motions and expressions.

"Come back and dance again," one of the women says. "Next time."

"We would love that," Eleanor says.

Eleanor and I have been a duo since day one, when I first became impressed with her knack for not fitting in.

It was during a layover in Atlanta, our first of four stopovers from Texas to Timisoara, Romania. A tall, spiky-haired boy was leaning against a beam in the terminal, preaching to a bunch of girls while our leaders were off buying Egg McMuffins for everyone. He wore Discman headphones around his neck and sunglasses on top of his head. His name was Tyler, and he was already everyone's favorite. Tyler looked a lot like the people who were on the brochures for this mission organization. He stood with ease, one hand stretched behind his neck, bicep flexed and elbow protruding. Ten girls surrounded him, including me, although I wasn't swayed by him. I could see he was attractive, but there seemed something plastic about him. I missed Danny and his goofy grin.

"Ladies, be the godly woman you are called to be, and the Lord will bring you a knight in shining armor, a strong warrior for Christ. Don't settle for anything less," Tyler said, flashing his straight white teeth. The girls leaned in closer and giggled. "But to get your knight in shining armor, you have to be worthy of his love. Not just a regular teenage girl. You have to be a princess in the Kingdom," he said.

"Awww! You're so sweet," one girl said.

"A princess of the Kingdom takes care of her body and works out. She reads her Bible and prays. She saves herself for her prince," he said.

I didn't think my body was up to princess of the Kingdom standards, and I wasn't sure I liked being called a princess anyways. I'm more of a put-the-worm-on-the-hook kind of girl. I'm a world changer, a Nazirite. Not a princess.

"You women are princesses, don't let anyone tell you otherwise. And I am a knight. It is important we give ourselves these titles because that is who we are in Christ," he said.

I was internally rolling my eyes when I heard a snort coming from the girl next to me. "Thanks, but no thanks," the girl said, her hands on her petite hips. Her cropped red hair swished when she spoke. "I'd rather just call us *guys* and *chicks*."

Tyler sneered at her. The other girls were silent.

"What's your name?" he asked.

"Eleanor. Eleanor Doyle," she said. Her voice was squeaky but loud.

"Well, Eleanor Doyle, God is going to have to work on your heart this month," he said.

Eleanor and I ended up being seated next to each other on the international flight. I told her in my most quiet voice that I loved how she stood up to Tyler. We gave Tyler a moniker—Godly Flirt—and we knew we would have plenty to laugh about with him around.

Somehow, Eleanor and I are considered the *rebels* of this trip, and I'm not even sure how that happened. We share headphones on long train rides across Romanian countryside, listening to Christian punk rock that isn't technically banned but highly discouraged because it doesn't draw us into the heart of worship. Also, Eleanor is a vegetarian, which is frowned upon in this group, because the Bible says we are to have dominion over the animals. Some of the other teens preach to her at the dinner table and try to get her to eat sausage. I am not sure how I feel about the issue, but I admire Eleanor for staying strong. Eleanor is the kind of person who loves Jesus but doesn't follow all the rules, and when I am around her I feel I can be that way too.

Still grinning from our impromptu dance party, Eleanor and I squeeze into our seats on our charter bus and share headphones. We stare out the window, watching flocks of goats and cattle graze on green rolling hills. I think about the Man with No Eyes and what it means that I haven't seen any miracles or any mountains moving. Our bus passes a Romanian man driving a horse drawn carriage. The man waves at us and we wave back.

I continue to pray for miracles every morning. I keep believing that God will do big things through us. I fill in the ink on my wrist every morning. *Here am I: Send me.*

On our final week of ministry, I'm studying these words on my body to try to distract myself from how cramped I feel on this public bus packed with a hundred Americans teens on our way to spread the Gospel and probably another fifty Romanians trying to make it to their jobs on time. I can smell the body odor and sweat of the people holding the wall handles behind me. *This is part of missionary life*, I proudly think. The bus driver is swerving around tiny European cars down narrow cobblestone streets. I am wearing drawstring cotton shorts and a Christian T-shirt that says "God's Hands and Feet." My hair is pulled into a thin French braid on the back of my head. I feel warm drops of sweat on my cheeks from the weight of my thick-lensed glasses.

I'm daydreaming about my dog back home when I feel something rough inside my underwear, moving around in circles. I don't realize for a few seconds that what I'm feeling is somebody's fingers. I whip my head back to find a skinny middle-aged man with large black pupils reaching up my shorts and fondling me.

"Stop! That's gross," I say, stunned. I don't know what else to say.

"Moolt," the man says, which is Romanian for *thank-you*. He pulls his hand out and slinks to another part of the bus and exits at the next stop about thirty seconds later.

Woozy and faint, I'm not sure what just transpired, and I'm not sure I want to know.

The girls who are huddled around me on the noisy bus haven't even noticed what happened. The bus keeps speeding down narrow streets, and my hair is still in braids, and the Americans around me are still laughing and the Romanians are still trying to get to work on time. The world is still going on around me, but something inside me has stopped.

We get off the bus and pass out tracts to the peasants feeding pigeons in the cobblestone town square. I pray with a toothless woman in a headscarf to accept Jesus. I play tag with some street kids who want their picture taken. They pose, giving each other bunny ears and flashing huge grins to show their gold teeth, as I snap photos of them with my disposable camera.

We eat at McDonald's for lunch. I order a Filet O' Fish sandwich as usual, which is crispier and more flavorful than McDonald's fish sandwiches at home. I sit outside with my teammates, eating my sandwich and drinking orange Fanta, shooing the pigeons away and watching Romanian teenagers sniff something from a paper bag. It's a regular day for us in Romania, just like the last twenty before. Except for this day, I can't shake the feeling of that man's touch on my body. The scratchiness of the fingers, the roughness of his movements. They keep playing in my mind over and over again.

I have to tell someone.

I approach my female team leader Taylor in our dorm hallway that evening about the man who assaulted me, only I don't use those words. I tell her someone *made a move* on me, and I explain that he put his hand inside my private part, careful not to be too graphic or inappropriate with my language. Taylor fiddles with her lanyard necklace that held the whistle she blew at the group during the day. Although my voice quakes, I don't cry. It feels strange to hear myself talk about it, almost like I am telling someone else's story.

"He came from nowhere, and then he was in my underpants," I say. "I don't know how he got there."

"I'm sorry that happened to you," Taylor says, but she doesn't look very sorry. She yawns and tosses her long brown hair behind her shoulders. At twenty-one, she is in charge of all the day-to-day operations of our trip, along with Caleb who is only twenty-two himself. They both seem worn out all the time.

"I can't stop thinking about what that creep did," I say. Now I am starting to tear up and my voice is getting loud. "He said *moolt*. That means *thank you*. Like I gave him something he enjoyed, or like I did something polite for him that he appreciated. Like holding open a door or letting him go ahead of me in line. . . ."

"Well, let's not get too emotional about this. What were you wearing?" she interrupts.

"Khaki shorts," I say.

"Shorts? Honey, you know you're only allowed to wear shorts on non-ministry days," she says.

"I know," I say, feeling embarrassed. I hadn't thought about the fact that I was breaking the organization's dress code. According to our handbook, repeated dress code violations could warrant getting sent home. Maybe I shouldn't have brought this up to Taylor after all.

"So that man was wrong to touch you, but instead of dwelling on it, maybe we can use this as a good lesson on modesty. As sisters in Christ, we have to help our brothers to not stumble," she says.

"Okay," I say. "You're right."

"If I had noticed you were wearing shorts earlier, I would have asked you to change. I take responsibility for that. But isn't it amazing how God can use bad situations to teach us things? He is so good," she says.

"Yeah, very amazing," I say, without feeling amazed at all.

"If you have any questions, don't hesitate to talk to me. I'm here for you," she says. She pats my knee, stands up, and says goodnight.

I lie in bed that night, trying to pray myself to sleep. I apologize to God for disobeying the dress code my leaders laid out for me, and ask God to help me forget what happened to me earlier that day. I fall asleep peacefully, but wake up in a sweat a few hours later from a dream where I am stuck on a bus in my khaki shorts, a legion of skinny men with dark pupils closing in on me.

Caleb summons us to the steps in front of the Orthodox cathedral in downtown Timisoara. I look up at the towering deep orange church with bright green triangle witch's caps. Even after seeing it every day for a month, I'm still enraptured by its beauty and disturbed by the darkness I sense inside.

"Today is the day," Caleb says. It's our last day of ministry, so of course today had to be the day. All month, Caleb has been talking about performing our drama—a three-minute reenactment of the crucifixion and resurrection to music—inside the Orthodox Church. This is our last chance.

"Before we start, I want to tell you guys something. I'm sure you've noticed those candles in the back of the church by now." We nod. "The Romanians use those candles to light curses on each other," he says. People gasp. "If that's not idolatry, then I don't know what is. That's why Jesus needs us to do this drama." My heart pounds with anticipation. We might not be smuggling Bibles in China, but we are going to perform a drama in a pagan church. I love mission work.

"We will trickle back in, not all at once. We don't want to draw too much attention to ourselves. We will be walking around like we are prayer-walking. They are used to that by now, so they won't think anything of it. I'll be in the back, setting up the speakers and cuing the music. We won't announce what we are doing, because the priest would definitely say no if we did. You guys know your parts by heart by now, so when you hear the music start up, find your places and go for it. It's a three-minute drama, and we really need to pray that the Romanians hearts are softened and that they see the truth in it. This is our last chance. You got it?" he says.

We nod again.

"You, you, you and you, go in first," he says, pointing to me and a couple of kids next to me. "The rest of us will wait outside and enter in small groups. Okay?"

"Got it," I say.

We walk around the ornate Byzantine-era sanctuary, laying our hands on the altar and various objects while muttering our prayers. Romanians around us are kneeling and praying in their church. My heart aches for their lost souls.

"Lord, let them see who you really are," I pray, extending my hands toward them. The tray of candles is flickering in the back, and one of the girls I came in with marches over to it, pulling me along.

"God told me to blow these out," she says.

"Really?" I say. I lean over the tray of flickering wicks and icons of the Virgin Mary and other somber saints I don't recognize. Wax drips down the sides of each tall white candle, deforming their shapes. Narrow plumes of smoke rise up toward the painted dome ceiling. I breathe in the warm, waxy scent that permeates the whole church. It's tragic that the Gospel is perverted this way, that these people think they have to use props to pray instead of bowing directly at the feet of Jesus. I think of these candles as the tools the Devil uses to distract these precious Romanians from having a personal relationship with Jesus. "Idolatry," Caleb said.

"Who will go for me?" the Lord asks.

Here am I; Send me.

A weathered old lady in a peasant skirt waddles up to the table with a fresh candle in her hands. She dips her candle into an existing flame and holds it for a moment, her eyes closed. Then she sticks the candle upright into a holder on the table, touches her left shoulder, and touches her right shoulder, her forehead and her chest. I wonder if she is praying for a blessing or a curse. She smiles, revealing toothless gums and looks to the ceiling, mumbling something in Romanian. And then she is gone, probably for a day of selling roses or eggs in the town square.

I can't take it. I want that sweet old peasant to know Jesus. I want her to know that prayer is a conversation, and cries to God can be expressed during the instrumental part of a praise song with guitars and drums, and that she didn't have to light a candle to talk to Jesus. I want her to know that real relationship with Jesus requires a lot more than a thirty-second prayer per day, that a true Christian partakes in prayer walks and intercession and fights as a warrior in the spiritual realm. I want to rescue her from her lukewarm faith. I want her to stop lighting curses on people. I want her to have what I have.

The girl from my team blows out the candle the peasant woman just lit.

"Only you, Jesus," she says.

Here I am; Send me.

I lean over a candle, shape my lips in an *o* and puff.

"Only you, Jesus," I say.

"Don't you just feel the Holy Spirit coming down on this place right now?"

"It's amazing," I say.

A few more of our teammates circle around the candle table and begin blowing out candles with us. Puff, puff, puff. Holy Spirit. This must be how Jesus felt when he flipped tables in the temple.

I am lost in euphoria over my bold stand for God when I hear a voice yelling in Romanian. A man in a robe is pointing to the door and corralling us out of the building like sheep.

"Go. Now," he says in a thick accent. This must be the priest. He follows us outside, where Caleb and half the team are waiting to enter. Through our translator, the man yells at Caleb. He's red-faced and talking with his hands.

"Your people are so rude, destroying the prayers of my people. Blowing out candles. Traipsing around my church all month long while my people are trying to pray. Touching all our sacred objects. Stuffing your faces with nasty sandwiches on my steps and laughing your loud American laughs," he says.

Caleb apologizes to the priest, a little red-faced himself.

"You are not welcome to return," the priest says, and turns back into the church. Our group is left on the steps, silent.

"Let's go," Caleb says.

We hang our heads and wait at the bus stop for what feels like eternity. No bus comes. We begin to walk the five-mile trip back to our compound. Caleb doesn't say a word the whole way. When we make it back with tired feet and spirits, he leads us to the field we worshipped in that morning.

"Drop. Fifty," he says. We all looked at each other. During our training week in Texas, our leaders warned that they would discipline us with pushups if they saw fit, but it hadn't happened with our team—yet. We stand around, dumbfounded.

"I said *drop*," he says.

I get down on my toes and began lifting my weight up and down over a patch of thistle.

One . . . two . . . three . . . four. . . .

The physical pain in my chest matches how I feel inside. I messed up our chance at ministry. How could I have been so stupid? I thought I was taking a stand for God.

Thirteen . . . fourteen . . . fifteen . . . sixteen. . . .

"Stupid kids," Caleb says, walking around to check on our form. "Now how are we supposed to reach people for God if we can't get in the pagan church? There goes our plan! Did you guys think of *that* when you blew out the candles?"

Twenty-seven . . . twenty-eight . . . twenty-nine. . . .

I beat my body, I make it my slave. I beat my body, I make it my slave. This verse in Corinthians is our mantra for the trip, but it never rang more true before now.

Forty . . . forty-one . . . forty-two . . . The Orthodox Church will keep lighting their candles, and they'll never know Jesus, and it is my fault.

Forty-seven . . . forty-eight . . . forty-nine. . . .

Fifty. . . .

I collapse on my belly in the weeds. Flattened, deflated, ashamed.

That night, Eleanor and I roll out our sleeping bags on the floor of our dorm room and talk late into the night. We leave for debriefing in Texas tomorrow, and soon all of this will be behind us—the man with no eyes, the man on the bus, the candles in the church, Tyler and his princesses, the women we danced with, the tearful prayers for the nations, the ways God whispered to us in the dew of the early morning.

I am unable to process any of this, but I do know how to laugh. So I laugh with Eleanor for release. We laugh until we are regular teenage girls again, not girls who came here to spread the Gospel, but just girls on sleeping bags, laughing, laughing, laughing. We call ourselves *rebels* because we are disobeying curfew. We laugh some more. Our dorm leader yells at us to shut up or she'd report us to our team leaders and get us sent home. We don't listen. Everyone is going home tomorrow anyway.

Back in Texas, we are given pep talks about maintaining our mission work at home.

"Keep up with your hour-long quiet times every morning, for the Word is our armor; don't dabble back in the sin you left behind, the world is just waiting to rob you of your joy. Witness to the person next to you on the flight home; if the plane goes down before they've had the chance to accept Jesus, you'll be held accountable."

I carefully take notes in my journal and embellish them with hearts and stars. "Pine Canyon is my mission field!" I write at the top of the page.

Tyler is collecting everyone's emails for some kind of accountability program he's devising, where women and men can get encouragement to be princesses and knights for the Kingdom. I opt out.

Eleanor and I say our goodbyes at the Dallas airport while waiting for our flights, mine to Sacramento, hers to Seattle. We hug. She fishes around in her backpack and pulls out the Christian punk CD we listened to every day together for the past month.

"I want you to have this," she says, putting the disc in my hands. "Don't forget about me."

"I won't," I say. I know I won't forget her, but I wonder if I'll ever see her again.

Seven

In the Sierra Nevada Mountains, rain and snow arrives every winter to fill the wild rivers and glacial lakes we swim in during the warm months. The rain comes to revive moss in the forests of pines and oaks and white birch. It seeps into the vibrant orange dirt so plants can grow and feed the deer, bears, and chipmunks. The two rivers that flow through Pine Canyon, the American and the Bear, rush throughout the summer, filling deep pools of clear mountain water with schools of brown trout lazily angling for a snack. In other places, the water spreads thin and white, moving briskly over beds of smooth granite and quartz. The region is a place that people from flat, dry places like Las Vegas or Kansas City only see on postcards. Tourists from San Francisco pay good money for guides to escort them down the American River in a raft; but those of us who live here never need to pay anyone, because the rivers are ours. My family knows the stretches that are safe, and we float down by ourselves in sturdy black inner tubes. On our way, we pass people fishing, panning for gold, picnicking, swimming with their dogs, and wading with their children.

But those of us at Pine Canyon Assemblies of God aren't deceived by outward appearances. We know we live in a desert, and that's why our youth group is called Voice in the Desert. Every Thursday night, we sing our anthem—a song about preparing the way for the Lord in the desert. We sing loud and off-key, swelling with all the gravitas of people who know they are God's voice to a dry and thirsty land. Often times in the summer, we hold our youth group meetings at the park, just a quarter-mile walk from church. We circle and hold hands under a sprawling buckeye tree, whispering prayers for revival.

"Jesus, bring revival to this land, this desert is thirsty for you," I say when it's my turn to pray. "They are thirsty for you, Jesus."

Trees, grass, and picnic tables surround the park's small metal playground, the same playground where I learned to climb and run as a toddler. A concrete pit is across the parking lot, a place that once was a sparkling pool I lay beside with friends after soccer practice, my fingers dyed bright red from the Skittles I bought from the snack stand. Behind the picnic tables is a basketball court with torn nets, where I once found a plastic egg with five dollars in it during a community Easter event. Those childish days are behind me. Now I come to the park to pray. It's a perfect spot overlooking the town, and at night we can see the flickering yellow lights of people inside their homes, people in need of God. We feel so big from this distance, looking out over tiny rooftops and treetops, like we can float above them all.

"Holy Spirit, Pine Canyon is crying out for you," Jacob prays. "And we cry out for Pine Canyon. Jesus, bring revival to Pine Canyon, right now, in the name of Jesus. Right now."

We sway together, interceding for our city, our cries to God getting louder and louder until the sun goes down and we feel a breakthrough from the heavens. We wipe our tears, collapse on the grass, and listen to the chorus of crickets in the background. Dahlia rises and challenges me to a race to the swings. I run after her, losing by a split second, and plop down on a swing, pumping my legs in the air.

"God is so good," I say, giddy from our prayer time and from the rush of air on my face as I propel forward on the swing.

"He is," Dahlia says, laughing.

"I've been dreaming about our destinies lately," I say. "I have a feeling they're going to be incredible."

Danny and a few other boys come by and snag our flip-flops from under our feet mid-swing, and run around, taunting us with them.

"Give those back!" I say, in a pretend angry voice. We jump off our swings and run after the boys, initiating an impromptu game of capture the sandal in the dusk. We pick up hard, waxy buckeye seeds from the ground and hurl them at the boys until they surrender.

It is on these summer evenings on park swings and parking lots under the stars that I am filled with a sense of wonder for my life and the God I worship. I am so bloated on hope I might burst.

We are setting up for a special show on a warm June night under a green gazebo in downtown Pine Canyon. A crowd of skater kids and a few guys smoking outside the Railhead Saloon are our potential audience. A warm breeze creeps through town as Kevin and Jacob test microphones and speakers. I'm huddled with the group, offering quiet prayers for God to speak through us, and gripping a white plastic mask from Party City at my side.

This is the first time we've performed *Masks* in Pine Canyon. We have done it in suburban churches, on soccer fields in Mexico, at the homeless shelter in San Francisco, but we haven't yet shared it in our hometown. We hadn't planned on doing it today, but when we were praying at youth group, God told us tonight is the night. He said souls were ripe for harvesting, so we packed up and came downtown.

Four of us line up on our gazebo stage in the blocking we rehearsed, and I embody my role as the promiscuous girl, and as I do I realize how much I miss doing theater. Kevin the sound guy cues up the music and presses play. The acoustic guitar music starts, and I begin silently blowing kisses behind a white theater mask. Paul is playing an angry man waving his fists in the air, Mark is playing a partier raising a celebratory glass, and one more kid plays a class clown busting up with laughter. We all are wearing masks.

Then, one by one we take the masks off. I go first. I bring my mask down to my chest, frowning and darting my eyes around in a face I hope would convey loneliness and insecurity. I catch a glimpse of our audience. The skater kids are laughing and poking each other. I feel a twinge of embarrassment, but remind myself their scorn will earn me jewels on my crown in heaven—the more persecution I face here, the more favor I'll earn in the afterlife. Besides, God wouldn't have sent us here tonight if He didn't have a plan. The other characters peel back their masks to reveal that the drinker is broken, the class clown is sad, and the angry man is scared.

Then the music amps up, which is Jacob's cue to come in. He gives me a gentle touch on the shoulder and motions for me to hand over my mask. I slowly place it in Jacob's hand with the perfect choreography we had practiced all summer. Jacob—who represents Jesus in the skit—gives me a side-hug and tosses the mask to the floor as I dance around it, free from my sin and shame. The drinker and the comedian do the same thing when Jacob approaches them, and get healed, but the angry man refuses and put his mask back on in the last stanza of the song. I have chills.

Jacob takes the microphone. "This is a story about finding our true identity in Jesus Christ and letting him take our masks away," he says, but the meager crowd is already dispersing. One of the skater kids sticks around for a moment and approaches us.

"Cool skit, I guess," says the skater kid, who is dressed in a denim vest with black-and-white patches of slogans I don't recognize.

"Yeah, dude. It *is* cool. Can we pray for you?" Jacob says.

"No, I gotta get back to my friends," he says, motioning his skateboard to the posse of guys who are walking away.

"Come check us out sometime. We meet on Thursday nights at the church on Grove Street," Jacob says. "I'd love to practice some tricks on our boards."

"Yeah, sure," the skater kid says as he begins walking away.

"What's your name?" Jacob hollers.

"Drew," he says, without looking back.

"We'll be praying for you, Drew," Jacob says. "Jesus bless you." Jacob turns to us and we know what we need to do. We hold hands and pray for Drew right then, that the Holy Spirit will speak to him in that very moment, that his heart will soften from our drama, and he will be compelled to hand over his masks to Christ. When we finish praying, we walk over to the Little Market and buy Mountain Dew and Sour Patch Kids. We take our candy back to the gazebo, which backs up to the antique red caboose parked in the middle of town. We sit on the gazebo's concrete floor and laugh about nothing in particular as the sun goes down and the downtown street lamps light up above us.

When we aren't reaching out to those in need, we are reaching deep within ourselves. Our prayer sessions in the summer go long and late, since none of us has school in the morning.

On one summer Thursday evening, my face is pressed on the maroon carpet again. Mildew fills my nostrils and I cough, launching a piece of mucus into the fibers of the floor. I don't move to clean it. Jessa is playing piano in the Spirit, and each of my youth group friends has spread out and found their own nook on the floor to break down the barriers keeping us from the Secret Place of the Lord.

"The only thing holding us back from being in the Secret Place is our own apathy," Jacob says.

I dig my face harder into the floor. I long to be in this Secret Place Jacob talks about. I want God to whisper privy information to me, to trust me with his divine revelations.

"Press in to find the Secret Place of the Lord. Press in, press in," he says. Jessa is humming and praying in tongues over us. "When we dwell in the Secret Place of the Most High, we are atmosphere changers," Jacob says.

"Atmosphere changers," Jessa softly sings behind him.

"We have the power to bring the atmosphere of the Kingdom wherever we go."

Atmosphere of the Kingdom.

"Jesus, let me dwell in your Secret Place," I pray into the floor. "Fill me with your atmosphere. Make me an atmosphere changer."

"You can change the atmosphere in your home by playing worship music," Jacob says.

"Change the atmosphere in our homes, Lord," Jessa sings.

"You can change the atmosphere in your car by praying in tongues as you drive."

Change the atmosphere in our cars, Lord.

"You can change the atmosphere in your classroom by soaking in the Secret Place before school."

Change the atmosphere in our schools, Lord.

"At work, you can change the atmosphere by prayer-walking the grounds during your shift."

Change the atmosphere in our workplaces, Lord.

I'm nodding into the floor.

Your Kingdom come, Your Kingdom come, Your Kingdom come, Your Kingdom come. We're dwelling in your Secret Place, Lord, we're dwelling in your Secret Place, Your Kingdom come, Your Kingdom come.

"Sing your own song to the Lord," Jacob says.

I sing, improvising a new melody, "in your Secret Place I live, in your Secret Place I live," but only the carpet and I can hear it. I feel something release as I sing. I feel like God is here, spooning me. God is a warm blanket wrapped all around me. I keep singing and the tears start flowing, as they always do when I press in long enough. They drip off my face and darken the carpet underneath.

I hear God whisper to me, "Welcome, Carly. Welcome to my Secret Place. Don't offend my Spirit and you can live here."

"Thank you," I whisper back. "Thank you, thank you, thank you."

"The Lord came down on us tonight," Jessa shouts. I pull my head from the floor and wipe my eyes. There is a dark splotch of spit and tears and snot where my face was, the place where God let me into his Secret Place.

Afterwards, Jacob and Jessa need to lock up the church, but the rest of us want to stay out forever. We are still glazed by the Holy Spirit. Dahlia suggests we go to Starbucks. After years of negotiations, Pine Canyon's no-growth planning commission finally has allowed a Starbucks to open in the old A&W Restaurant building by the interstate. It opened yesterday, and we couldn't be more excited. All of us atmosphere changers jump at Dahlia's idea and pile into cars headed for the most happening new spot in town.

Once at the store, I'm overwhelmed. I stare at the menu for five minutes, unable to pronounce anything. "I haven't had coffee before," I say to the barista.

"Get a Frappuccino, like maybe the Java Chip Frappuccino. It takes like a chocolate chip cookie," the barista says.

"Okay. I'll have one of those," I say.

I hold the plastic cup in both hands, toying with its long green straw before daring to take a sip. I've never been interested in coffee before; the smell of Mom's Folgers makes me gag. I hate it when she spills it in the car and it dries in the cup holders. In an act of bravery, I bring the straw to my lips and taste. *Oh gosh, that's good.* I take a bigger taste, and then a gulp. I'm sucking it down and using the end of my straw to lap up the whipped cream and chocolate chunks.

The caffeine hits my bloodstream in minutes. I squish with my friends on an overstuffed leather couch in the corner. We are slurping our drinks and crumpling up torn pieces of newspaper from a basket near the couch and throwing them at each other. I'm laughing at everything that's said. I can't help it. Everything is funny.

I pick my cuticles in the moments between jokes.

This must be what it's like to be kids from the suburbs, I think. Curling up on a leather couch, drinking five-dollar sugary coffee drinks from regions of the world we can't pronounce. To the untrained eye, we look like regular teenagers, I think: hyper, flirtatious, loud, loiterers of coffee shops. We aren't dressed in long skirts or suits, like the Mormons, and we don't carry Bible tracts in our pockets. My short, pixie-cut hair is dyed bright red from a box. The other girls wear makeup and dangly earrings. The guys use gel to spike their hair. Yet we know we are nothing close to average, because we have something the rest of the world can only dream of. We live in the Secret Place of God. We bring the atmosphere of the Kingdom to Starbucks.

The barista, whose skin shines with oil, kicks us out when the store closes. She bends over to pick up the pieces of newspaper we've thrown on the floor. None of us is ready to go home. Not with the Spirit and caffeine surging through us. We step outside. The stars are bright tonight, the air is fresh. We turn the keys in Dahlia's car just enough for our song—"Dancing in the Moonlight"—to come on. We know it's not a Christian song but it's featured in the movie *A Walk to Remember*, which is sort of a Christian movie. We turn up the volume.

"Let's dance," I say. I grab her hand. The boys roll their eyes and move to a different part of the parking lot, embarrassed by our dancing as usual.

We sing, bumping our hips together and lifting our hands in the air. Dancing in the moonlight. I can't imagine anyone else in the world is happier than we are right now.

Danny and I are raking leaves for a family of the church that owns a large piece of property on the canyon, a job that many of us church kids do when we need some extra cash. Danny isn't carrying his weight on the job today, but I don't care. I'm just so thankful to get some one-on-one time with him.

"What would you do if I turned into the Hulk right now? You're just raking leaves and you turn around and I'm totally green and grunting," he asks, leaning against his plastic rake.

"Does that mean we'd get this job done faster?" I ask.

"Well, I'm the Hulk, I think that should go without saying," he says.

"But what if the Hulk doesn't care about raking leaves? Maybe he'd rather, like, go kick down that shed over there," I say, pointing to a dilapidated wood structure.

"True. Actually, I kind of want to kick down that shed over there right now."

"Don't. Forget I said it."

"Danny is HULK," he says slow and grumbly, lumbering toward the shed.

I sigh, but I'm stifling a laugh. Physical labor is not Danny's thing. He talks a lot, tells a lot of jokes, takes a lot of breaks, and has a hard time concentrating on the monotony of scraping the ground of debris. Danny is meant for more than raking leaves.

"Is it lunch time yet?" he asks. I check my phone—it's only 10 a.m.

"Sure, why not," I say, feeling bored from the work myself. We sit on a giant tree stump overlooking the river, eating the sandwiches we packed. The river from this distance looks like a painting, its rapids frozen in time and so quiet. I look out at it, loving this moment between us.

"I have some big news for you," he says. My heart stops, like it does when anyone ever says they have *big news*. "The Nazirite preacher invited me to work for him," he says.

"You mean . . . *the* preacher?"

"Yes. I know, just hear this." I have a mouthful of ham so I nod. "He picked me. Out of thousands of people, he wants me."

"But his church is in Los Angeles."

"Yep. I leave next week."

"Next week?! That's so soon." All of a sudden I can feel the tree stump's sharp edges poking into my tailbone.

"I know. When God moves, He really moves. It was crazy how this all worked out. I wasn't even looking for a job. Isn't that just so Jesus, though?"

"How did he find you?"

"We met at the Candlestick Park revival, remember that one?"

"Yeah." Apparently when I was wandering the stadium with the other lukewarm kids, Danny was meeting *the* preacher.

"He said I have a special calling over my life. We got to talking, and I mentioned that I do graphic design. He tracked me down through Pastor Frank and called me last week," he says. "He needs someone to design his brochures and church website."

"That's . . . that's incredible," I say. I'm letting the reality sink in that in a week, Danny will be living at the opposite end of the state. Danny lowers his voice.

"I won't forget our little church, you know. I've learned so much here, and I'll miss everyone. I'll never be able to replace you guys."

"We'll never be able to replace you," I say, trying not to cry. As we rake leaves together the remainder of the day, I work with a sense of urgency. I need to soak up this time with Danny. It's all coming to an end.

Nine days later, Danny's Geo Prizm is packed up with all the belongings he will take to his new life four hundred miles away. Tonight we are gathered in the park to say goodbye. Jessa brings big, soft sugar cookies from the grocery store, and a few quilts for us to sit on in the grass. We huddle around Danny. "Jesus, go before Danny in this new season of life," Jacob prays.

"Jesus, we ask that you would spread your love through our friend Danny," I pray. Danny is nodding and agreeing with us in the Spirit. We pray until we know Danny is covered and ready to be sent off. Then we linger for hours in the grass under a crescent moon, and as the evening creeps past 10 p.m., people trickle off, saying their good-byes to Danny with bear hugs and high-fives and play punches in the gut. Jessa asks me to bring her quilt to church on Sunday. Kevin is the last to leave, and I can tell he doesn't want to leave us here alone.

"You guys should get home soon," Kevin says.

"We're fine, Kevin, see you later," I say, and it comes out sharper than I meant it to.

Kevin starts up his Thunderbird, watching us even as he peels away. Finally, as I've hoped for all night, it is just the two of us. We lie in the grass of a softball field, talking about God's destiny. I've been imagining this moment for days.

"So, you're off," I say, wishing I could say so much more.

He turns to face me. "There's something really special about you," Danny says. "It's like God's got you marked."

I bask in his words, my heart beating fast. *God's got you marked.*

"Like in what ways?" I ask, prodding for more. *Tell me I'm beautiful, like you did the day we first met.*

"It's just who you are. You're real, and it's so refreshing. God is going to use that spirit of yours, I know it," he says.

"Thanks," I say, grinning wide. Not beautiful, but real. I'll take it. "I think it's awesome how you're following His will for your life."

There is a pause, and Danny tosses me a volleyball we played with earlier in the evening. I toss it back to him, and we play catch on our backs. I want to freeze the moment in time so I can stay forever, but the minutes tick on, and I know my parents will worry if I stay out much later. Reluctantly, I stand up, brush myself to stall for more time, and say I need to go.

"You have time for a quick swing, don't you?" he asks.

"Of course."

Danny starts his car, which is parked just a few feet from the swing set, rolls down his windows, and turns on a worship CD. We kick up our legs on neighboring swings, our toes piercing the air in front of us, higher each time. In the short time I've known Danny we've shared countless times of prayer, revival, fasting, and laughter. The Holy Spirit wrapped us tightly together for a time, and now it is time for him to go change the world. I understand that. Still, I am not ready to let go. God directs all our paths, so this must be part of

God's plan, even if I don't like it. I've spent time in prayer over the last week, trying to surrender my heart, which I've been told is deceitful above all things.

"Crazy how God brought me here," Danny says. His red hair is flopping as he flies forward on his swing. "I mean, this time last year, I didn't even know Jesus."

"And now you're called away."

"To help spread the revival."

"So amazing," I say, trying to mean it.

Our rusty swing chains are creaking louder as we pull harder on them with each kick forward. We are swinging in synch, flying up and down at the same speed.

"I want to keep in touch with you, if that's okay," Danny says.

"I'd love that," I say. "You know, I have family in Southern California. I could come visit you sometime."

"That would be beyond awesome."

Now Danny is swinging higher than me, and our motions grow out of synch, despite my futile efforts in flinging my legs into the air to keep up. "You'll be hearing from me," he says. Danny kicks his heel in the sand beneath us to stop his swing, and I do the same. He holds up one large freckled hand in an invitation to a high five. I meet his hand with mine, but instead of slapping and moving away, I let it linger. We sit on our swings, which are still reverberating motion and squeaking, our palms pressing against each other's. He smiles at me, his pointy chin jutting out from his ruddy face. There, on the swings, our palms touching, I am overwhelmed with this sense that we are sitting on the cusp of revival. We believe it will happen, this revival, and although we don't know what it might look like, we have faith beyond sight. We believe if we pray a little longer, or worship a little louder, we will see the revival enkindle in our desert land, in our generation. This promise illuminates everything.

Tonight, we aren't just a boy and a girl on swings; we are two souls on the verge of seeing Jesus do something incredible. I imagine this revival, whatever it is, should begin on a summer evening just like this one, where frogs croak, and the air is cool but the sand beneath us still warm, and a boy is almost holding my hand.

"I'll miss you, Carly," he says. I swoon.

This is the closest thing to romance I've ever had.

Eight

"Who are they?" Jessa asks, pointing to the poster over my bed. "Those are The Beatles," I say, trying to hide my shock that Jessa doesn't recognize them.

"Oh, The Beatles. I've heard of them before," Jessa says.

"Most people have," I say. It came out a little more sarcastic than it sounded in my head. This is Jessa's first time at my house. I'm having a little youth group party, and I've been excited to show Jessa my room, since I've been in hers so many times.

"They don't look like they love Jesus," she says.

"The Beatles? I guess they didn't. Or I mean, maybe they did though, you know?" I say.

"I don't think so, just look at their faces," she says. "I didn't picture you having a poster like this in your room. You come across so pure and godly at church."

Have I been hiding something from Jessa?

The poster is my favorite Beatles photograph. It's the one where the four of them are looking into the distance, their scruffy hair slightly blown by the wind. John and Ringo are showing off bushy sideburns. Paul is ducking his head over Ringo's shoulder with a slight smile. The other three look serious. For my fourteenth birthday, my brother gave me a 12x36 version of the photo in a white wood frame to match the black-and-white hues in the portrait. It is the best gift I've ever received. I've recently repainted my room bright yellow with sponge prints of lime green hearts, pink stars, and orange flowers. The poster doesn't match at all, and I don't care one bit.

"That's, um, an old poster. I forget it's there," I say. I cringe a little. I'm lying to Jessa—I study the photograph every day. I love it.

"Remember what we're learning about atmospheres? I don't think this poster is helping the atmosphere in your room," she says.

"Ha, yeah," I say.

"Why so frowny, Mr. Beatle? Was someone mean to you? Or are you sad because you don't know Jesus?" she says, in a mock baby-voice while pointing to John.

"That's John Lennon," I say. "He isn't alive anymore. He was shot a long time ago."

"He's dead? It always makes me sad when someone dies without loving Jesus," she says, turning her eyes away.

"We don't really know what he believed," I say.

"The Bible says we will know them by their fruit. Did John Lennon have fruit?"

I've known that secular music is bad for a long time, and I hardly listen to it anymore, except the Beatles. I can remember when I first learned that Satan is the Angel of Music, at Missionettes three years ago. Satan was the Lord's favorite angel until he rebelled against God, got kicked out of heaven, and opened his own dark Kingdom. That's why rock music can be Satanic, because it is within Satan's domain. I remember once asking Mom if John Lennon was Satanic and if he went to hell when he died. She said of course not, without looking up from the onion she was chopping. I didn't press her answer at the time, because I liked it. I don't like to think of John Lennon suffering. I don't like to think of anyone suffering.

But now Jessa is implying that John Lennon *is* in hell, and that my poster of him is ruining the spiritual atmosphere in my bedroom, and I think she might even be a little disappointed in me, which crushes me.

"I don't know . . . I guess not," I say.

Kevin the sound guy pokes his head in. This is also his first time at my house, and I don't like how conspicuously excited he is to be here.

"Hi, Kevin," I say, relieved to be interrupted from this conversation with Jessa, even if it is by Kevin.

"I uh, picked an apple off your tree and ate it. It was so good," Kevin says. "I can't believe you grew up out here, it's just incredible." His khaki pants have a mud smudge on them near the pleats. He scans my room.

"Wow, Carly, did you, er, do all the sponge painting yourself here?" Kevin says.

"Yeah," I say, looking at Jessa. She is still flustered by the Beatles poster.

"This is impressive. I mean, I wouldn't have picked these colors. Geesh, it's like we're in Willy Wonka's room." He makes a disapproving grunting noise, and covers his eyes as if my room is too much for him to handle. "You have some real talent though. Wow."

I hate Kevin and Jessa right now, in my space, disapproving of me, belittling me. And I want to punch Kevin . . . *real talent?* It was the easiest thing in the world to cut out shapes from big sponges and press them against the wall with paint I found in Dad's shed.

"Hey, why don't we go see what everyone else is doing?" I say, jumping off the bed.

I try to brush off my talk with Jessa on my bed but I can't. Every time I see the poster I feel more convicted. Jessa is right: their faces look so lost.

A few days later, I hear a voice as I try to fall asleep.

Take it down.

That's the Holy Spirit, I think.

Then I hear Jessa's voice. *They don't look like they love Jesus. Remember what we are learning about atmospheres?*

But God, I'll read my Bible longer each day.

Take it down.

I'll only listen to Christian radio in my car.

Take it down.

I see Jessa's face when she first saw the poster in my room. The way her smile dropped, the way her eyes looked so heavy. *I'll take it down for three months*, I think. Just three months. I flip on my lamp, stand on my bed, and lift the poster off its nail hangers. It's heavier than I remembered. I carry it to my closet, swallowing the hard lump in my throat.

My phone rings at 11 p.m. on a Wednesday. It's from an area code I don't recognize.

"*Carly!*" the voice on the other end shouts. I pull my ear away from the receiver, but I'm grinning because I recognize the voice. It's him, Danny McKeller.

"How the heck have you been?" I ask. It's been a month since he left for Los Angeles and I never thought I'd hear from him again.

"Oh, Holy Mother of Buzz Lightyear, I have so much to tell you," he says. He has so much to tell *me*. He has been thinking about me.

"I want to hear it all," I say, and I do.

"Oh, Carly, I wish you could see what God is doing down here. It's just crazy, indescribable stuff," Danny says. His voice is hoarse.

"Do you have a cold? You sound different."

"Ha, no! I've just been praying nonstop and evangelizing, so my throat is sore." Danny has settled into his new job working for the church and God is blowing him away, he tells me. I listen and try to match his enthusiasm. "Get this. Yesterday afternoon, I met a man at the donut shop, and he seemed really down, so the Lord asked me to talk to him," he says.

"That's amazing you can hear the voice of God like that," I say. I think about how I heard the voice of God recently too, about the Beatles poster. I remind myself to tell him that story when he is done with his stories.

"He told me his whole life story. He served time in prison but now he's a landscaper."

"What an open door to share the Gospel."

"Yeah, I know. Anyhow, I told him about Jesus, and the Holy Spirit came down on us right there at the donut shop, so I took him back to the church and met up with the rest of the college group, and we stayed up all night praying and feeling breakthroughs."

"Wow. Amazing."

"Carly, you've got to get down here and experience this. I want it to change your life," he says. I remember something else to tell Danny too, something that will show him that I have been having breakthroughs here as well.

"Cindy invited me to join the worship team," I say.

"*Woot!*" Danny says. "Talk about the favor of God on you!"

I tell him the whole story, that Cindy took me to the cramped church kitchen after service to tell me something important. Danny knows what an honor this is, the highest honor at Pine Canyon

Assemblies of God. Cindy takes her worship team very seriously, and the only way to make the team is to be personally invited. And the only time Cindy invites someone is if she feels led to by the Lord.

"She said there are people with better voices, but they don't have my heart."

"Wow," Danny says, and breaks off into a wild laugh. I tell Danny about my new spiritual responsibility to lead others into the heavenly court. I tell him about the quote from Pastor Frank that Cindy passed to me with the statement of faith I signed to begin practicing with the worship team: *Your life should uphold the hands you raise in church.* Danny says the quote is powerful, just as I hoped he would.

I don't tell Danny that my invitation to the worship team hurt Dahlia's feelings, and that my heart breaks for her to be left out of something she wants so badly. I can't focus on Dahlia's disappointment right now; this is the most exciting time of my life.

When my family takes a trip to visit our extended family in Southern California, I make sure to incorporate seeing Danny. I thought I'd get to sneak in a quick visit between other plans, but it turns out Danny gets along so well with everyone that he hangs around us all week, eating my grandmother's lasagna, playing Taboo with my cousins, joking around with my brother. On the last day of our trip, we ride canoes on a nearby lake and end up brown from head to toe from a serious mud fight. Although we talk about God and pray some, we don't do any evangelizing, and I don't see the miracles he told me about on the phone. But it feels like a miracle to me. When it's time to say goodbye, he pulls me in for a hug and makes me promise to come visit again.

I ride this high through the remainder of the summer, when, for a week-long mission trip, our youth group goes to Juarez, Mexico, to perform *Masks*, share our testimony, and play games with the kids on the street. I feel the Spirit move through me in Juarez as he does during worship.

On our last evening in Juarez, Heather and I are relaxing on the swings at the playground outside our cinder-block dorm compound. The sun is hanging low in the sky, and we've been reflecting on how the Spirit moved through us that day. Heather and I still aren't best friends, but we are the only two girls on this trip—we have to stick together.

The leaves in the trees around us begin to rustle and a chill runs down my spine. A breeze picks up, and the sand underneath our feet blows around in circles. An empty cigarette pack flops by. An eerie feeling is sweeping over me. I've heard scary things about Juarez, but I never felt afraid until now. If I ignore the feeling, maybe it will go away.

"This is creeping me out a little," Heather says. I look over at Heather in shock. It's like she's reading my mind.

"Me too," I say. "Seriously, I was just thinking that."

"We have the Holy Spirit, though; we don't need to be afraid," she says.

"Right," I say.

We hear a screech, and then a bigger gust of wind picks up a white plastic grocery bag about twenty feet away. It twirls upward before it catches a current of wind heading our direction. The bag flies by us, brushing my ankles. I yelp, kick the bag away, jump from my swing, and run. Heather follows me. Once inside, we hug and catch our breath.

"There was a demon in that bag," I say.

"I thought the exact same thing," Heather says. "There was definitely something very evil going on out there. Let's go tell Pastor Frank."

I have heard about sinister things happening in the spiritual realm—a realm that Pastor Frank says is more real than the one we can see—but I've never actually seen it in real life before. We find Pastor Frank and Cindy praying in their room.

"We sensed something demonic outside," Heather says, before I can open my mouth. I give her a dirty look. I am shaken up but proud of my spiritual intuition, and I was hoping for some recognition for it. Heather is making it sound like the demon is all her idea, which irritates me. I want credit. After all, I saw it first.

"We are not surprised," Pastor Frank says. "Cindy and I are sensing some dark spiritual warfare tonight, and the Lord has asked us to be relentless in fighting against it. I am going to have to ask you to stay inside the rest of the evening, and to tell everyone to do the same. I'm proud of you young ladies for coming to us with this."

We go warn the guys about the demonic forces around us. Jacob has stayed back at the revival tent to minister to a local man who recently gave his life to Christ, so the guys are on their own. They are sitting in a circle on the concrete floor of their dorm, playing poker and betting with the leftover candy we brought to pass out to kids. I wonder who brought the contraband playing cards. If Pastor Frank knew they were doing this—oh, we don't have time for that right now. We have news to deliver.

"You guys, we got a really creepy feeling when we were outside just now, and Pastor Frank says there is evil in the atmosphere, and he's praying it away," I say.

"Not surprising. It's probably because we're playing Texas Hold 'Em," one guy says, and a few other guys snicker.

"We're serious!" Heather says.

One of the guys, Mark, jumps up.

"I have to go pray with them," he says.

Heather and I walk back to our dorm room, shut the windows, and sprawl on our bunk beds listening to worship music on our Discmans. I fall into a fitful sleep in my jeans and dirt-stained T-shirt. At some point in the night, the wail of a siren awakens me. Drenched in sweat, I pray myself back to sleep.

The next morning, as we eat our last meal together in Juarez, Pastor Frank looks pale and glassy-eyed as he silently sips a mug of chamomile tea.

"Frank and I were up all night praying for everyone," Cindy says, tickling his hairy arm with her fingernails. "He was looking out for all of us. Mark was with us too, bless his heart. Who knows what evil our pastor saved us from."

Pastor Frank isn't ready to talk about it yet.

"I heard a siren last night," I say.

"I know, honey. That could have been the force of evil we were praying against. Perhaps the police caught it before it got to us," Cindy says. I wonder if Pastor Frank saved me from being murdered or kidnapped. What would have happened if he hadn't stayed up all night praying? I am eternally grateful.

I tell all this to Danny on our next talk on the phone, not forgetting to describe the emptiness of Pastor Frank's eyes the morning after the incident, how he had depleted all of himself to protect us.

"What kind of leader does that?" I ask Danny.

"The kind I want to be someday," he says.

We talk about his new college group and all the incredible things they are doing for the Lord. They do prayer walks around the city and fasting weekends and homeless ministry. It sounds like he is settling in wonderfully. I'm happy for him but jealous.

He asks to pray for me over the phone. "Jesus, I ask that you would awaken the beautiful Spirit of my friend Carly," he begins and

I curl up on my bed and smile. I love it when he prays for me. He is still praying when my cell phone dies at two in the morning. I fall asleep with the phone pressed against my cheek.

I can't fall asleep. There is something heavy in the atmosphere of my bedroom and my stomach is lurching just like it did when I saw the demon in Mexico. I lie in bed, holding my breath. I make sure to cover every inch of my body with my lime green comforter to hide from the presence.

This presence is wispy and invisible, yet weighty and portly. It isn't more than a foot tall but it weighs a thousand pounds. These are just estimates, because I haven't got a measuring stick nor have I got a good look at it. But it's here, for sure. It hovers over my face and tries to get me to break. I turn over and lie with my face to the pillow. It kneels by the bed and grunts in my ears. I curl into the fetal position and plug my ears.

"I'm gonna get you," the presence says.

"No, you're not, because I have authority in Jesus Christ," I say.

"Ha-ha, you're funny when you're stupid. I'm going to get you, you'll see."

"Jesus, you have power over the Enemy," I say and begin to pray in tongues. And with that, the presence dissipates into the atmosphere.

I lie there, thinking about what just happened. Jacob has been talking about the curse of generational sin, and it all makes sense to me now. The demon in my room is from the sin of my parents and grandparents. Mom grew up Christian but rebelled and spent some years as an alcoholic before finding Alcoholics Anonymous, while Dad was raised by his Polish mother in Chicago after his Irish father decided he'd rather drink and read history books than be a dad, and all of their sin is conglomerated in this creature. Only through intense Spirit-filled prayer can I break these chains.

I set to my mission by turning typical family outings into my spiritual battlefield. When Mom and Dad suggest a day at the river, I agree, knowing I'd have to put on the full armor of Christ around them. I'm not thinking of this too much though when I'm at the bank of the American River, cold water rushing around my feet. My ankles are numb, and the sun on my shoulders feels wonderful.

My back is leaned up against a granite boulder. I am underlining passages from a book called *Unlocking the Power of Prayer*. I stopped reading novels a year or so ago, turning all my attention to the Bible or spiritual development books, because I know if I am not getting closer to God, I am falling away. I heard that in a sermon once and it stuck with me. My brother is reading something by J.R.R. Tolkien. He's been to all the same revivals I have, but they didn't stop him from reading novels.

Later, we eat a meal of corn on the cob, cherries, and grilled chicken on a wooden picnic table a few yards from the water, our dogs milling about at our feet, waiting for morsels to fall from our plates. We don't pray before eating like the people from church do. As we eat, Dad tells a story about some old derelict gold miner he met on the river that day. I push around my food on my plate, sulking. I wish my family were more Christian. Next to us, the river rushes constantly, filling the spaces between words.

As the sun sets, we play Rummy by lantern, the game we always play. Mosquitoes whine in our ears as we hunt for runs and three-of-a-kinds from the discard pile. I wonder if I should start abstaining from playing cards to be a witness to my family. Pastor Frank doesn't allow anyone to play cards at church functions, not even games like Crazy Eights or Slapjack, because he says it can open doors to the

Spirit of Gambling—but I think that would only invite more questions from my family.

I wonder what Pastor Frank and Cindy are up to tonight. Probably praying together, or worshipping around a bonfire, or dissecting passages of the Bible around the dinner table. Meanwhile, all my family wants to do is play cards at the river. I long for the kind of family with a spiritual legacy, the kind Jessa talks about at youth group. As we scarf down blackberry cobbler for dessert, I am struck with the sense that I am to be a voice to my family, the Desert.

Some of us from youth group have started a band called Kleerside, named this because we are on the godly side of life where everything is clear, not murky and confusing like life would be without Jesus. Dahlia is our lead singer. I sing and play piano (I play just enough to clunk out basic chords). My brother plays the electric guitar, and two other guys from youth group play the bass guitar and drums. We write and sing songs about pursuing God, resisting temptation, and loving Jesus, and we practice once a week at the church before youth group each Thursday.

Today when I arrive early at the church for practice, I find Pastor Frank, Cindy, Jacob, and Jessa sitting around a table in the sanctuary.

"You might be wondering why we are here. We wanted to hear about this band of yours," Pastor Frank says, tentatively. "What's the name again?"

I freeze. Maybe we were breaking a rule by not telling them about our band first thing. "Well, we are called Kleerside because we strive to be on God's side in everything we do," I say, carefully choosing each word. The other people from the band aren't at practice yet.

"That's wonderful to hear," Cindy says. "Because you know that piano is anointed for worship. Jesus wouldn't want any ungodly music coming from it." The piano is a high-end electric Clavinova, and the church shelled out a big chunk of their annual budget for it a few years ago. They made the investment because a good piano is key for deep worship experiences. I guess Cindy needs to make sure the Spirit of Secular Music does not defile her Clavinova. I understand this, especially since I am on the worship team.

"Oh, definitely. We only play Christian music," I say, which is almost entirely true. Last week we jammed to a Beatles song but that was only to warm up. The music we *write* is all about God.

"It can be Christian but still not God-honoring. It depends on the spirit you guys are playing from," Jessa says, piping in.

"Yeah that's for sure," I say. "We soak with the Holy Spirit before every practice so I think God is in our music." We usually do pray before practice. I don't know if it is long enough to be considered *soaking*, but the pastors look at each other and nodded approvingly when I say this.

"Oh good," Pastor Frank says. "We are so proud of you young people. We weren't suspicious of you, we are just looking out for you guys and our flock. It's our job as your leaders."

"Oh yeah, we understand. We appreciate that you care so much."

"Well, Jacob is going to watch your practice today," Pastor Frank says. "Cindy and I have to get going, but Jacob wants to see what you guys are all about and hopefully give you our blessing."

My bandmates start filtering in, and we start practice, with Jacob as our one-man audience. The others give me looks that say, *why is he here?* and I smile and shrug my shoulders. I can't let on that I'm nervous.

"Why don't we start by playing 'Unbound'?"

"Unbound" is a song I wrote recently, and I think Jacob will like the lyrics. I sing into the microphone and raise one hand in worship. My eyes are closed, but I'm peeking occasionally to see if Jacob is smiling. He's not. He is taking notes on a Steno pad.

We're unbound
From this world we live in
And we'll do anything
To get others believing
Wash away the thoughts inside, yeah
That keep my mind away from You

Jacob claps when we are finished. "When are you guys going to perform in church?" he asks.

Later that night, I'm lying on my bed, staring at the glow-in-the-dark plastic stars on my ceiling I arranged into the Big and Little Dippers. I'm thinking about the day. Why did we need Jacob's blessing? Why did it feel like I was in trouble, even though they said I wasn't? Why do they care so much about what kind of music we play? *They are trying to protect us*, I tell myself. And their instruments. They are trying to protect their flock from sin. I get it.

Then why do I feel this way?

It's been thirty days. I know because I'm counting. Thirty days since I've listened to the Beatles. I've given up all other secular music, but the Beatles are so hard for me to go without. I've been going strong, and I even bought some Christian CDs that are supposed to sound like the Beatles. I don't think they sound anything like the Beatles.

I dig through my disorganized heap of CDs and find *The White Album*.

We're unbound from this world we live in.

I hum "Unbound," as I study the list of album tracks. Track Seven: "While My Guitar Gently Weeps." My favorite Beatles song. I want to listen to it so bad.

Wash away the thoughts inside, yeah
That keep my mind away from You.

But I won't. Tomorrow it will have been a month, and then it will be easier. I decide resolutely that I won't, and then in a flurry of hand movements and button-pressing my muscles remember, I'm hearing that haunting electric guitar opening. George Harrison's voice flows from the tiny speakers on the stereo I've had since my twelfth birthday.

I'm not sure why I love this song so much. I can't say why it hits me the way it does, but it moves me in a way that nothing else can. Tonight, I listen to it and cry. I don't know if I'm crying because the song is beautiful or because I've failed God.

Tomorrow I will start at zero again.

Nine

I'm in the back room of the pizza parlor at the start of my shift, holding a vase with a single white rose. There is a note with my name on it attached by a piece of twine. I unfold to see a sketch of two bulgy-eyed penguins jumping off a glacier.

This job might be the worst, but it's great fun when you're around, the note says in messy writing. I look up and catch Marco watching me read the note as he tosses a ball of dough in the air. He winks. I take the rose and the drawing and hide it behind a tub of sliced mushrooms in the walk-in refrigerator so our co-workers won't see it. I turn on scalding water to fill up the stainless steel sink and let the steam rise up around me.

Marco can't like me. He's kind and funny and smart, and even cute with his floppy brown hair and flushed lips. He knows my favorite flavor of ice cream and is studying economics at the community college. We are close in age. When I speak, he listens like I have important ideas and important stories. And he can draw. Marco can't like me because he isn't a Christian, so I can never date him, no matter what. No matter how sweet he is or how many penguin pictures he draws me or how much we laugh together. I scrub pizza pans with a ferocious vigor as I think about what to do.

That Thursday at youth group, I confide my temptations in Jessa.

"I've been having feelings for someone," I say. Jessa and I are in Pastor Frank's office with the door closed.

"Who?"

"Well, that's the problem. You don't know him. He's not a Christian. I work with him."

"That is a problem," she says, opening her Bible. "Funny you bring this up. I thought you and Danny had something special," she says.

She noticed that? Did everyone notice it?

"Oh. Danny and I are . . . just friends," I say. The truth is, I would drop everything for Danny. But Danny doesn't give me flowers or ask me about my day the way Marco does. And Marco is close to my age, and lives in my town, and of course I want to wait for Danny, but I am being tempted along the way. I want to say all of this, but I don't. Jessa is already flipping through her Bible.

"Well you haven't acted on your feelings for the non-Christian yet, have you?"

"Oh, definitely not. I have to admit I've thought about it though."

"Honey, I can't understand why you would struggle with feelings for someone who doesn't share the closest thing to your heart. To be honest, this surprises me, Carly."

"I know. It's not like me at all. But you would understand if you met him. He acts a lot like a Christian, actually. He's really kind and patient and nice."

"But we know his heart isn't for Jesus. I'm so glad you came to me."

She begins reading from the Bible out loud:

He who dwells in the Secret Place of the Most High
Shall abide under the shadow of the Almighty.

I will say of the Lord, "He is my refuge and my fortress;
My God, in Him I will trust.
Surely He shall deliver you from the snare of the fowler
And from the perilous pestilence.
He shall cover you with His feathers,
And under His wings you shall take refuge;
His truth shall be your shield and buckler."

I close my eyes and pretend to be thinking deep spiritual thoughts, but I am confused as to how this passage is relevant to my situation. Jessa reads it again, this time replacing the pronoun "you" in the chapter with "Carly," so that it reads like a personal proclamation from God to me.

Surely He shall deliver Carly from the snare of the fowler
And from the perilous pestilence.

I guess Marco is the perilous pestilence?

"Can you commit to memorizing the whole chapter with me?" Jessa asks. We spend the next twenty minutes memorizing the first five or so verses in the chapter. Jessa says with Scripture in my heart, I will be protected against the temptation.

I've memorized most of Psalm 91 when, a few weeks later, Marco and I are sitting cross-legged on one of the restaurant's red plastic tables after closing, trying to throw parmesan cheese packets into an empty cup on another table. I toss one, aiming carefully, and I make it in the cup for the first time.

"Nice," Marco says. He gives me a high five.

"Yeah, baby!" I say.

I take a sip of my Dr. Pepper and look down. This is the first time

Marco and I have spent time alone. Maybe I shouldn't be here right now.

His truth shall be your shield and buckler.
He shall cover you with his feathers.

"I'd love to take you on a real date," Marco says.

My eyes meet his, those big kind brown eyes. "I'd love that," I say. I didn't think about it. I didn't pray about it. I didn't seek counsel. I am saying exactly what I want to say in this moment.

The next evening, I'm sitting next to a cute boy in a dark theater with Tom Cruise on the big screen and I'm trying to enjoy what I know is supposed to be a milestone in the life of any teenager, but I'm feeling like I'm making a huge mistake.

We are at *The Last Samurai* at the Cineplex in a neighboring town. Marco passes the popcorn and I grab a handful, brushing wrists in the process. The hair on my neck stands up. I want to hold his hand, but I am scared to. And he hasn't made the move to hold mine. This confuses me; I thought all non-Christian boys want to get physical right away.

Midway through the movie, Tom Cruise is running around training to be a ninja or something, but I can't focus. I am obsessed with the memory of a sermon illustration I've seen before involving blue and pink construction paper hearts. It was last year, at a purity conference. An anonymous-looking youth pastor with a goatee and pierced ear held up two construction paper hearts, one pink and one blue.

"This is what happens when you date someone," said the youth pastor, and he glued the two hearts together. "Oh, isn't it nice! Happy feelings! Kissy kiss! Boundaries fly out the window in the heat of the moment with your hottie." We all laughed at this, and nodded along. "And this is what happens when you breakup." He ripped the pieces of paper away from each other, leaving two torn hearts; pink scraps were left on the blue heart and blue scraps were left on the pink heart. The youth pastor paused, letting us marinate in the power of the moment. Then he came back with a low, whispery voice, "Is this the heart you want to present your future spouse?"

I cannot get that line out of my head tonight, nor the image of the broken, shredded paper hearts. I clench my shoulders and sit stiffly in my theater chair. That dilapidated heart could be me after just a few more foolish choices. When Marco hugs me goodbye at the end of the evening, I make sure to pull away before any Elmer's has the chance to set.

I give this a lot of thought over the next few weeks, but the right choice was clear from the beginning. I can't go on another date with Marco. I do decide that maybe I can witness to him instead. As the only true Christian he knows, isn't that my responsibility? Nothing in Psalm 91 says I can't witness to cute non-Christians. So I invite Marco to the corn maze with my church group, and he accepts, saying he'd love to get to know my friends.

We meet up at Starbucks. Candace brings her new boyfriend along. Rumor has it this mysterious man she's been seeing is a Baptist, but Candace assures everyone that he has a great heart for the Lord, despite his Baptist ways. I am skeptical. Candace is one of the first people who introduced me to going deeper with the Spirit, and now she is yoked with someone who doesn't practice it himself. But Candace has seemed so happy lately, with less serious talk and more hair twirling and smiling, so that's good, I guess. And I can't judge—after all, I am the one bringing the non-Christian boy tonight.

People introduce themselves to Marco but then ignore him for

Candace's boyfriend, whom they all adore right away. He plays with Candace's hair and teases her just the right amount, not like a jerk, but like someone who is fond of a person's quirks.

"She always wants to meet at Starbucks, and then she orders *apple juice*," the boyfriend says. Everyone laughs. The mood is so festive it's like they've forgotten that the boyfriend is a Baptist, and the boy I brought isn't an *anything*.

Everyone but Jessa, that is, because Jessa knows of my temptations more than anyone else. When we climb into the back of Jacob's car, Jessa dives to the middle seat between Marco and me. She leans into my ear.

"I would not normally sit this close to a man who is not my husband," she whispers. "But I'll do anything to protect you, Carly."

I nod and utter a "thanks," but I wish that I could have sat next to Marco. Not just because I like to be near him, but also because he doesn't know anyone in this group, and I don't want him to feel uncomfortable.

"I've been listening to these sermons on CD," Jacob says as we settle on the dark, windy road to the corn maze. "Whoa. They are life changing."

"Tell them about all the fasting," Jessa says. "Carly, you're going to love this."

Marco looks at me and raises the corners of his lips, like he is asking my permission to laugh. I look away.

"This man, he fasts until he sees a miracle," Jacob says. "He has sold all his possessions, quit his job, and prays full time. What an act of faith, right? And the thing is, the Lord always provides for him. He's even brought someone back from the dead. It's just incredible, incredible stuff." He swerves over the double yellow line.

I lean over Jessa to see Marco. He is staring out the window and his face is white. He must think this is so weird. I would too, if I didn't understand it. I try to change the subject.

"Jacob, are you excited that snowboarding season is coming up?" I say. I don't care at all about snowboarding, but I know Jacob loves it, and so does Marco. Maybe that will help them connect.

But Jacob doesn't hear me, or pretends not to. He isn't done talking about the Miracles Guy. I wish he knew that Marco isn't a Christian. Or maybe he does know, and that's why he is talking about this stuff, to witness to him. If this is witnessing, then I am a terrible witness. Marco knows that I go to church and believe in Jesus, but that's about it. I never talk to him about fasting or miracles or radical acts of faith. I stay away from telling him that stuff because I don't think he would understand it. And just maybe, I'm ashamed.

"Jesus told his disciples to leave their mothers and fathers to follow him. I've been thinking about what that really means, if we were to take Jesus at his words." Jacob's boldness both embarrasses and convicts me. I'm certain he's going to scare Marco away.

At the maze, I am so worried Marco isn't having fun that I have no fun myself. We pay ten dollars each to wander through dead cornstalks in the dark and feign concern about being "lost." Jacob leads the way, carrying an orange plastic flag so we won't lose sight of him. The rest of the group hangs back, following Jacob through the night and talking about God without paying attention to where we are going. People are saying things like "God has been telling me . . ." or "I feel led to . . ." or "I've been praying about . . ." I keep looking up at Marco to see his reactions. He cocks his head and raises an eyebrow—we must look like freaks to him. I wish my friends would talk about their jobs or their pets or anything else. Can't they ask Marco about what he likes to do? Can't they dial it down for one night? At least while we're at the corn maze?

I do nothing to ameliorate the situation. I care about what Marco thinks, but I care about what my church friends think more. So I agree and nod along with their talk of God—without adding anything myself—because I can't bear them thinking Marco is making me backslide. *I have to act the same way I would if Marco wasn't here,* I tell myself. This is an example of not being ashamed of the Gospel. Still, I can't relax.

Afterward we go out to eat. Some people from the group order pancakes and French fries under the diner's fluorescent lighting, but all I feel like is herbal tea. I need something to settle my stomach.

"So what church do you go to?" Jacob turns to Marco. This is the first time someone has spoken directly to Marco all evening. There's a pause, and Marco looks at me with big pleading eyes.

"Marco doesn't have a church," I say. And then, because I see the wrinkles in Jacob's forehead crease, I add, "Yet."

Marco looks down at his pancakes and Jacob studies him.

"Jacob, honey, can you tell Kevin about the sermons you've been listening to?" Jessa says.

Kevin looks at me with his bulgy eyes. Jacob starts talking about the fasting and the miracles all over again.

Marco puts my $1.50 peppermint tea on his tab, and I fight him in front of everyone just to prove that we aren't together like that, but the waitress is walking away with his debit card already, so I mumble my thanks.

This will be the last time I see Marco, I decide. I can't bear Jacob's disapproving looks and Marco's confusion. Marco is a nice guy, but he lives in a different world than mine, and I can't straddle them anymore, even if my goal is witnessing. I need a guy who is immersed in my world and pushes me further into the things of the Lord and listens to the same sermons as Jacob.

I miss Marco in the weeks following, but I tell myself it's for the best. With him out of my periphery, I can focus more on God again. I feel I owe Jesus extra passion and focus after being so distracted by Marco. My morning devotional time—or "pressing in" as Jacob calls it—begins to grow longer and longer.

One morning, my knees are smashed into the carpet of my bedroom floor, making squiggly red imprints on my skin. My feet are numb. I've been going strong for two and a half hours, praying against generational sin and demonic atmospheres, and am going to keep going until I feel a breakthrough.

The door to my bedroom flies open.

"What are you doing in here? Why aren't you doing your school-work?" Mom says. She is standing in the doorway with one hand on her hip. Her other hand is holding a steel mixing bowl. Her hair is a mess.

"I'm spending time with Jesus. Do you think school is more important than Jesus?" I say.

"Just wrap it up please," she says, and shuts the door.

I feel like crying. Jacob says to expect this kind of resistance when we start to change atmospheres, but this is hard. My relationship with Mom is getting tense, and I feel like so much is unsaid between us. I long for her to understand what is important to me. She has been proud of my mission trips and passion for God in the past, but all of a sudden she is pushing back on my devotion. She encouraged me to go to this church, and even attends herself now—but she isn't up to the spiritual caliber I want her to be. When she talks about God, she uses the words "love" and "grace" a lot, which sounds like some kind of hippie-dippie faith to me. Of course I believe in love and grace, but it has to be balanced with holiness and devotion. People should be fasting and denying themselves and pressing in to see miracles. I begin to pray for both Mom and Dad to see revival in their own lives. But this only seems to make things worse.

One night after youth group, Mom swarms me with her usual questions from the kitchen.

"What was it about?" she asks.

I hate these questions from Mom, especially about youth group. Doesn't she know that youth group isn't *about* anything? The Voice in the Desert isn't some topically themed childish Bible study. As if Jacob sits around on with cookie-cutter lesson plans and says, "Okay, kids, today we're going to talk about Jesus!" No! We are igniting our generation for the Lord. Mom's very question of "What was it about?" shows me she has no concept of the deep spiritual warfare we are fighting.

"What was it *about*?" I ask, rolling my eyes. "It was about revival. It was about the Spirit. It was about being radical for Jesus."

"I'm sick of you. You can go to your room," she says.

I stomp off to my room and slam the door. I push my pen down hard on the pages of my journal.

My mom is TERRIBLE, I write. *She doesn't understand me.*

As I write, though, I start to wonder if maybe I'm not mad because Mom doesn't understand me, but because she does. The truth is, I don't know what youth group is ever about. I shudder at the thought.

I'm so tired. I want to quit all of it and hide. It's too much, I write.

I want to curl up in Mom's lap and tell her I'm scared. I want to tell her I might not believe in the kind of God who needs all this from me, or any God at all. I want to ask her if I can go back to working on my tan with Jane and reading novels by the river. I want to go to the movies with a boy without losing sleep for days. I want to fall asleep in Mom's arms and wake up years from now when I'll have everything figured out.

But I can't do that. That would be giving up. I didn't snub Marco for nothing, and I'm not standing up to Mom for nothing either. Besides, she's not exactly inviting me to her lap. She acts like she's disgusted by me half the time, or that she wishes she had a different daughter.

That's fine. I wish I had a different mother.

There is a spiritual realm around me more real than the one I can see. Evil is immanent and it is up to me to break its chains.

I'm in my car in the parking lot of the pizza parlor, waiting for Danny. He is late, which doesn't surprise me. He's visiting his mom for the holidays and has a lot of people to see during his short trip, but told me over the phone that he really wants to make time to see me. Our plan tonight is to go for a drive, and stargaze at this parking spot he knows about.

For Christmas yesterday, I received an album from Mom and Dad called *Rumours*. Even though I don't hang out with Marco anymore, I allowed myself to keep one of the mix CDs he gave me, which I of course keep secret from Jessa. I feel so guilty, but I can't help myself. Secular music will always be my weakness. My favorite song on the mix CD is this one about growing up and falling down a landslide. When I first heard it, I was so struck that I had to show it to Mom. She said it was by a band called Fleetwood Mac and they have a lot of beautiful songs.

The landslide song doesn't look like it's on this album, but there are twelve other songs I've never heard before by the band. I tell myself it's okay to listen to because it's a Christmas gift from my parents. I'll go back to breaking chains of evil after the last of the Christmas ham is gone.

I pop the CD into my car stereo and I watch raindrops run down my windshield as I listen. I think about my collection of Christian music, and wonder why it can't sound like this. At first, I keep checking the time, anxious for Danny to arrive. But as time passes, I start to settle in and relax to the music. I kick back my seat and close my eyes.

A song called "Silver Springs" opens with the same rich voice from the landslide song. Stevie Nicks, the album's flap says.

The song is quiet but building slowly, and to what I'm not sure. Nicks's sweet, warbling voice is gaining grit . . . more and more . . . and now she's belting out this angry crescendo like she's righting every wrong she's politely endured. I don't know how the song makes me feel, but it makes me feel. It's like the singer is growing up in the middle of the song, and she's taking me with her through this change from little girl to strong, fierce woman. I tap my steering wheel and watch my windows fog over.

I'm wrapped up in this transformation, in this unleashed power coming from my speakers and this strange feeling is washing over me when a knock on my frosted window startles me. Danny hops in the passenger seat and I scramble to press "off" before he can hear it.

"What you listening to?" he asks. The music stops.

"Oh nothing. I mean, not nothing, like *nothing* nothing, just nothing you would like," I say. I'm rambling. The feeling—whatever it was—is gone and I'm back to being excited to spend an evening with Danny McKeller. This is the night I've been waiting for. I tune into our local Christian radio station, where I not only know the songs will be about Jesus, but will stay within the range of feelings that are safe to share with Danny.

The feeling, as I begin to refer to it in my mind, was too wild and unkempt for the Carly I want to show Danny. The feeling made me like a different girl . . . different woman. *But never mind the feeling for now*, I tell myself. Tonight is about Danny and me.

We drive up and down back roads behind the home where Danny grew up to find our lookout, but the clouds are too thick with rain to reveal any stars.

"Let's go back to my Mom's house and warm up," Danny says.

"That sounds wonderful," I say, and I mean it.

He leads me to the brick fireplace at his mom's and motions for me to sit. He hands me a fleece blanket and asks his mom to make us his favorite hot cocoa. "I'd love to, Danny," she says, smiling at me. I wonder if she thinks I'm Danny's girlfriend. I wonder if I *am* Danny's girlfriend.

"I feel God is pressing in on me," Danny says, pushing his hands on his chest. Clinking sounds are coming from the kitchen and crackling sounds from the fireplace. The blanket I'm under is warm, and I'm thinking how natural this all is, how I could spend night after night here, with Danny and his mom, talking about the mysteries of God.

"Me too. He feels so near to us," I say.

Danny's mom brings us the hot cocoa on a tray with two silver spoons. She seems like an entirely different person than the woman who cleaned her purse in church last year.

"I'll be upstairs," she says. "Holler if you need anything." She winks at Danny.

I instantly feel a desire to impress Danny's mom, to have her approve of me as the girl Danny brings home for cocoa and for his grandmother's gold ring. I don't know if his grandmother has a gold ring, but if she does, I want to be deserving of it. I want to talk to Danny's mom about clothing and our bodies and what takes our breath away. I watch her grab a book off the coffee table and walk away.

"Your mom is so nice," I say.

"She is," Danny says. His eyes are distant.

It's quiet for a moment, and I remember the feeling I had earlier today. I want to feel that way again soon. I'll play the song, or maybe another song, and I'll see if I can get the feeling back. I'll think about it later. For now, I'm sipping hot cocoa with a man who loves Jesus and maybe me.

As the gray month of January trudges along, I listen to a lot of Fleetwood Mac, but I don't get the feeling again. Instead, I cling to the memory of the warm fireplace and ceramic mug at Danny's house and wait for my phone to light up with his calls. He calls two or three times a week through the spring, always late at night, always about revival and divine appointments and Jesus. By April, our conversations begin to wipe me out. I feel like I can't keep up with his intensity, but I wouldn't dare bring up a trivial, unspiritual topic like what I had for dinner. I remind myself of something that Jessa told me once, that intimacy is never comfortable.

One night in June, Danny calls later than usual, but I am up waiting for him. He sounds wired. He says he heard a sermon about destiny today and he wants to help me find my calling.

"God has a destiny for you just waiting to be unlocked. He marked it on you when you were born, and it's something that only you can do," he says.

"I want to find that destiny," I say.

"Here's how you find it. When was the last time you cried?"

"Um, let me think."

A few days ago I cried when I finished the last page of *Angela's Ashes* by Frank McCourt as optional reading for my English class. I hadn't shed a tear the entire book, until my eyes rested on the white space under the final paragraph. I read the last page again, this time barely being able to see through the blur of my tears. I cried for all the poverty and alcoholism and family dysfunction and the resilience and hope and beauty in all of it. I don't know. I didn't think about *why* I was crying when I did, and I still can't put it into words.

"Just this book," I say. I mention the title. He hasn't heard of it, which doesn't surprise me. There is a lot of swearing and a few sexy parts he wouldn't approve of.

"And what about the book made you cry?" he asks.

"I don't know. There was all this unspeakable sadness in it, but also so much hope. Our spirits have this strength, you know? And it was written so beautifully, it just got to me I guess," I say. I realize how stupid I sound as I talk.

There is a pause on his end. "Hmm. Interesting," he says. "The things you cry about, those are the things that reveal your heart's tender places. And your heart's tender places reveal your destiny. I'm not sure how the book relates to that," he says.

He's disappointed with my answer. I panic and feel like an idiot for trying to talk about *Angela's Ashes* with him. He was trying to help me find my destiny and I just blabbed about some book I enjoyed. What else can I say that will sound more spiritual?

"I cried during worship recently too. Just thinking about how amazing God is," I add. Danny grunts and it sounds like he's lost interest in the conversation.

"Well, keep praying about why you cried in that book, and maybe God will reveal something to you. I gotta go, though," he says.

He hangs up the phone in record time, and I know I blew it.

Something is going on with Danny. Our conversations are still about the Fire of God, but the spark in his voice is gone. I miss the

Danny of the Sleeping Bag Wars, and the late night park rendezvous and the mud fights. I miss the Danny of no windshield wipers and the *woots* and the loud laugh.

Maybe I could bring back that side of him if I see him in person. We could talk the way people in love do, not just about revival and the Fire of God, but about our feelings. He could hold my hand as we talk about our destinies, or maybe we could just go to the movies. I start planning my trip. I invite Paul, and Eleanor Doyle—who I've kept in touch with by phone since our Romania trip and who is flying down soon to spend the summer with me—on a road trip to Southern California.

I arranged to meet Danny at his church on a Friday in late July. We hit the road early in the morning to make it to the church in time for a prayer-walking session. We had dropped off our bags at my grandma's and visited briefly before heading out to see Danny.

Despite everything I've heard about this church, I wasn't prepared for seeing it. I park and gape; a dozen palm trees and twenty pillars line the entrance to a four-story glass-paneled church building. There, by a gold sculpture in the likeness of a Great Blue Heron shooting water a dozen feet high, I see him. He's leaning against the fountain in cargo shorts. His shape is rounder than I remember, and there is a new patch of dark red wiry hair on his chin, but it's definitely him. My heart feels like it might explode from my chest with each step closer. I run to him, throwing restraint to hell. This is *Danny* we are talking about.

"Danny!" I shout from twenty feet away. He turns to face me and smiles big.

I leap at him and reach my arms up toward his neck. I dangle from him for a moment in the most wonderful hug I've had. I want it to last forever, but Danny puts me down and pulls away.

"Hi Carly," he says, but there is something faraway in his eyes.

"Danny!" I repeat stupidly. "Danny, I'm here! I'm finally—"

"Carly, I'd like you. . . ." he starts. He grabs the hand of a girl I hadn't noticed standing beside him.

"—I'd like you to meet Lisa," Danny says. Lisa is probably some friend from his college group. That's so nice of him to include her tonight, I think. He's introducing me to his friends. That must mean he's talked about me to them.

"Lisa is my girlfriend," he says.

My legs go numb and I steady myself on the fountain. This can't be real. This is a joke. No, he couldn't have said that. I imagined it, I think. But the words are still ringing in my ears. *My girlfriend.* I can faintly hear Eleanor introducing herself to Danny and the girlfriend, and Paul and Danny high-fiving. Conversation swirls around me but I am watching it from inside a glass tank. It's faded, blurry, distant.

Play it cool. You have to play it cool.

How long has he been with Lisa? That's her name?

"Let me give you a tour," Danny says. He leads us inside the church. It's a giant opera-house-style auditorium with arched ceilings, chandeliers, and onyx-plated walls with gold detailing. *When he called to help me find my destiny, was he with Lisa then? Or is that what made him go to her?*

"This place is so anointed," Danny says, waving one arm around the dark sanctuary. His other arm is linked with Lisa. This is the church where all the supernatural things happen, all the divine appointments and miracles and touches of the Spirit Danny has told me about for the last year. It all feels like a charade now. *When we drank cocoa by the fireplace at his mom's house, was he with Lisa then?*

We walk by an intercessory prayer group in session in one of the church classrooms. They stop praying to give Danny and Lisa hugs. They ask us to join them in a prayer walk around the church.

"Let's do it," Danny says. "I brought my prayer warrior friends, right, Carly?"

When he prayed for me, saying my name in that way I loved, was he with Lisa then?

Danny prays out loud as he leads us around the church campus, that the Spirit's presence would wash over it like a flood. He doesn't stop touching Lisa. He takes us to a rectangle reflecting pool, where about fifty church interns are gathered. Danny introduces us to twenty or so of them. I shake a lot of hands.

"Look, it's Pasadena's cutest couple!" one of them shouts and brings both Danny and Lisa in for a hug. So other people know about Danny and Lisa. Does Lisa know about me? Danny suggests we all go out to dinner together, and I agree because that is what someone would do if her heart were perfectly unbroken. I'm playing cool.

We order omelets and curly fries at Denny's in downtown Pasadena. Eleanor chats with Lisa and learns she is in the middle of taking a year off from work and school to pray and rest. I study her as she talks. She is the height of a meerkat and about as skinny too. Even her voice is small. Next to Danny, she almost disappears. Her hair isn't anything special, but it is clean and styled pretty. As she talks, I picture her and Danny kissing, cuddling, praying together. Because she doesn't work or do anything except pray and rest, I imagine her following Danny around, leaving fresh-baked banana bread on his doorstep until he noticed her, ensnaring him into her mediocrity. But she doesn't seem desperate that way. She looks so content with her small body and small life, like she doesn't need to prove herself to me or anyone else. I hate her for no other reason except that Danny picked her instead of me.

Danny talks about the miracles he's seen lately, and the ways

God is moving in his life as I pick at my chicken sandwich. He is droning on about transcendent experiences and the power of prayer, but I am not listening. There had never been anything between us, I see it now. It was a fantasy, just like the fantasy of revival I prayed so hard for. Revival only made sense when I was in love.

"Call nine-one-one!" a man's voice shouts and I'm yanked from my thoughts. Danny is so busy talking about revival, he doesn't hear. Our waiter runs to our table and yells louder.

"We're on fire. You all gotta scram," the waiter says.

Customers are fleeing their tables. The restaurant fills with smoke and it stings my eyes and lungs. I hear a siren in the distance and it's getting louder. I grab my purse, check to see that Eleanor and Paul are with me, and run out of the building.

"Wait!" a voice shouts.

Smoke is swelling out the front door and I wave it away with my hands to see who is talking. I think it's the diner's manager.

"You have to pay for your food!" he says. "You can't just leave."

The fire department pulls up and five firemen jump out and pull out a thick hose from the side of the truck.

"Move, people, fire department here," they say.

"Make a line right here to pay for your food," the manager says.

"You're in the way," the fire department shouts.

"Stand over there," the manager says.

So I stand at a busy street corner in Pasadena at midnight with Danny and Lisa and a bunch of people from their church I don't know, and there's a fire inside and I'm going to pay for an uneaten sandwich, and I'm wondering what I'm doing here. I want to bolt down the street and never come back.

"Why do we have to pay for a meal we didn't finish? It's not our fault the kitchen caught on fire," Paul says.

"We are spreading the Gospel by being good customers," Danny says, and I nod even though I have no idea what he is talking about. One by one, we reenter the smoky restaurant to cover our tabs. I drive us back to my grandma's house without saying a word. Eleanor and I get in our pajamas, brush our teeth, and shut off the light to the bedroom we are sharing with Grandma's stuffed bears and antique books.

"Goodnight," she says.

"Night." The air is so quiet but my mind is on full throttle. I'm trying to think sleepy thoughts when it hits me like a knife to my chest.

"Oh Carly, what's wrong?" Eleanor asks. But I can't speak. I'm sobbing like we do at the altar, only nothing is spiritual about this cry. I'm just a girl crying for a boy now. Was it ever something more? Eleanor rolls over and holds me. She strokes my back.

"Oh, Jesus, Jesus, Jesus," she says.

"I . . . liked . . . him . . . so . . . much," I say, between heaves.

"I know," she says. Only she couldn't have known because I never told her. I never told anyone. She prays for me and plays with my hair and lets me cry. We fall asleep like this, and when I wake up a few hours later with a yelp and more cries, she starts to pray again. She doesn't use a lot of big words, she just says, "Jesus, Jesus, Jesus."

Ten

Mom is unpacking the ice chest she brought to our friends' cabin in Tahoe. We are borrowing their house for a little family get-away on the lake, and everyone is getting along well. Our family has always loved Tahoe.

Paul's phone rings. It's one of his friends.

"Uh, guys?" Paul says, hanging up the phone. "There's a fire in the canyon." Dad immediately starts pacing the house, overreacting as usual. He takes off the straw hat he only wears on vacation and throws it on the counter. It's August in California, I want to tell him. Fires happen all the time. I just hope it won't get in the way of our vacation.

"I gotta get in there," Dad says. His reaction scares me. What does he mean "get in there"? Does he mean leave Tahoe and go back home? It's just a little fire, right? The firefighters will put it out, and then we can go to the lake and laugh about all of this.

But then I think about our two dogs trapped in the house that we left for a neighbor to care for.

"The van, the dogs," he says, grabbing his keys. The van with all his work equipment. Maybe he should go, just to be safe.

"I'm coming with," Paul says.

"It's not safe," Mom says, clutching a bottle of ketchup with both hands. My stomach clenches and I have to remind myself to breathe.

"I'm going," Paul says.

They run out of the house, and I hear the car's engine rev up as they back out of the driveway. I find a nearby bedroom, climb on a bed with a log cabin quilt and a carved pine nightstand, and start to pray while picking at the threads on the quilt. *God will protect us. I am a Nazirite and my prayers matter. God will stop this fire in the name of Jesus.* This is my chance to act in faith.

Mom's phone rings. I run out to hear who it is.

"They've got the road closed. The whole hill is evacuated. They're not letting us in," I can hear Dad's voice over the receiver, his words blending together in one slurred breath. "We gotta hike in."

He hangs up. Everyone evacuated? Roads closed? Hiking in? *Oh God, hear my prayer.* My phone rings. It's Dahlia.

"Are you okay? Are you safe? Is your house okay?"

"I don't know," I say, realizing I don't know anything right now. I promise Dahlia I'll keep her updated and then I go back to claiming victory in the Spirit over the fire. I command the flames to die in the name of Jesus. I quote Scripture, "Ask anything in my name." I remember the parts of the Old Testament where God protects the righteous and I claim those over the fire. I pray all the ways I've been taught, all while trying to shake this feeling that it's too late.

Hours later, Dad and Paul come back with his work van, shaken and covered in ash, along with our two dogs Molly and Steven.

"We could see flames from the kitchen window," Paul says. With all the roads closed, they had hiked through the canyon to get to the house.

"It was like an oven in there," Dad says. His voice is cracking.

Reports online, which are several hours delayed, say the fire has spread over six hundred acres and is ten percent contained. I'm pacing the house now too, along with everyone else. Mom keeps sweeping the same square of kitchen linoleum. We don't even go to the lake—we stay inside, glued to our phones and the television.

The eleven o'clock news comes on, and Caroline Carter, the Sacramento news anchor I remember from childhood, calmly tells us the fire has burned through a thousand acres and that one structure is destroyed. When she says "one structure," the screen flips to footage of a swing set in flames, the kind that are sold at Kmart in the summer. The smoke rises up and around the swing set, but I recognize its candy cane stripes in the three second clip. Then the screen switches to a heap of mangled burnt metal and wood that I don't recognize with my eyes but I do recognize with my gut. The newscaster's voice continues over the clip . . . "The cause of the fire is undetermined."

Dad turns the TV off.

"Enough of this," he says. Mom is still sweeping the kitchen and Paul is playing guitar quietly. That was our house. None of us say it, but we all know it to be true.

I think of how Caroline Carter said "one structure," in that sterile voice, how she didn't use the word "house" or "home," or a "place where people love and fight and stick together to carve their little spot in the world," and she didn't call it a "barn that one family spent a lifetime dreaming and ten years building," or even a "place where a little girl used to play on a swing set." But I can't expect Caroline Carter to know any of these things. These are all things that only we know, the four of us in a cabin living room with our rescued dogs and our unspoken fears.

The rest of the family goes to bed, but I stay on the couch, waiting for another newscast. At 3 a.m., the network runs a rerun of the eleven o'clock news, and I again see the candy cane striped swing set and the pile of rubble. Sometime after that, I drift to sleep. I wake to a call from the fire department confirming what we already knew.

Dad and I spend the day like zombies watching infomercials on the tiny TV in the Tahoe cabin, staring at the screen in a catatonic trance for hours, our eyes bloodshot and wet. We take turns breaking down with tears, but we hardly speak.

The Red Cross calls in the afternoon, telling us they have set up shop in the Pine Canyon Community Center and have "resources" for fire victims. When we visit the center the next day or so, I take a second helping of gummy worms and two boxes of animal crackers from the snack table. After all, I am a *fire victim*. At least that's what everyone keeps calling me. The fire is big news for Pine Canyon. People all over are talking about us. Pictures of our flattened house are on the front page of all the local papers.

"It probably started from a spark from an illegal camper on the river," the fire marshal says.

I instantly hate this man, both the fire marshal and the camper whom I've never met. A *spark?* The guy was camping on the river. Maybe throw some water on the damn *spark* and stop a thousand acres of trees and my house from burning. I'm not even sorry for mentally cussing. *Damn.* It doesn't mean anything anymore.

Early the next morning, three firemen escort us to our property. Pastor Frank is here too, because he thought we would need him. But he's not the usual Pastor Frank; he's quiet, maybe even mournful. We turn the corner of our dirt road and the view opens to a vast stretch of black char and mangled trees.

"It's like Mordor," Mom whispers from the front seat.

Three days ago, this was our home, and now it's a pile of disfigured debris. Well, two piles of debris. One for the trailer, and one for the Barn—we never stopped calling it that.

The oak trees I climbed as a child are flipped upside down, their gnarly, crisped roots exposed. My lungs are itchy from the hazy air. Smoke still rises from the mess.

"Be really careful," a firefighter says. "It'll be smoldering for weeks, probably."

Ashes are fluttering above us in the sky.

I thought in coming here, I would find some treasures. Maybe God preserved my prayer journals as a testament to his faithfulness, I had secretly hoped earlier this morning. Something like that would happen in the Old Testament. Wouldn't that be a story to share at church? The journals would be sitting on a glowing gold pedestal, and the fire department wouldn't be able to explain the miracle.

My magical thoughts dissipate as I take in the pile of blackened metal around me. I think I see a dilapidated iron stove, a contorted chimney, and a melted bathtub. Or at least I think it's a bathtub. It's in the spot the bathtub was. None of the house's walls or floors remains.

"It's not real!" I cry. "It can't be." I step over a bunch of broken glass to the area I think may have been my room. "It's not real," I say, but saying it doesn't make it any less real. There's nothing I can say to make this different. I can pray and shout and scream, and none of it will change. I squat and piece through the grime, hoping to find a remnant of my old life.

The Beatles poster, I think, and my heart seizes. I want my poster. Or maybe I want to go back three days and put the poster back up so it can burn up where it belongs, not in the closet, but framed above my bed in all its beautiful, melancholy glory. My poster didn't deserve to burn in the closet.

I let out a yelp. The grief is a physical stab and I buckle under it. A fireman approaches me and hands me an iron stick. "To protect your hands," he says. I poke around the grime with the stick but all I find is a couple of deformed marbles from my old collection. I keep them.

That week, I am quoted in the local papers about how sad I was that my dad had just built a deck. I don't remember saying that, but I doubt we gave them anything quotable. Dad hates the picture of himself looking over the black canyon on the front page. My parents aren't the type to enjoy attention.

The newspaper stories draw even more phone calls from concerned people, and I learn to use these conversations to perfect the correct language and posture of a fire victim. I relay the story to people, giving them enough details to make them feel special, and openly grieve with them on the phone for a few minutes. Then they offer to pray for me, and when they are done praying, I say things like "I know God is in control," or "God can use this for good," or "Everything happens for a reason," even though I'm not sure I still believe those things.

I am really trying, but it's hard now.

On Sunday, eighty-four hours after we got that first call from the fire department, Cindy dedicates a song—"In Christ Alone"— to my family during worship. Over and over we sing the chorus about how we can proclaim Christ in every victory in our lives. Over and over we sing the chorus as the tears flow from my eyes to my chin to the floor. I want to believe it so bad, and I think if I sing it louder I can.

After service, Kevin the sound guy brings me a journal with Scripture written in the inside cover and a note that says I can talk to him anytime. He stands there, as I read it, waiting for my response.

Cindy interrupts to give me a hug and leads me outside.

"Frank and I prayed about this," she says, tucking a piece of my hair behind my ear. "And I want you to know that after we soaked in the presence of the Lord, God told us this tragedy has nothing to do with your sin or your family's sin. Sometimes bad things just happen. God isn't punishing you."

"Of course I know that," I say, wiping tears from my eyes. But was that something other people were thinking? The thought hadn't even crossed my mind. I picture Frank and Cindy discussing my family and deciding if the fire had to do with our sin. I've been so busy grieving I forgot about generational sin. I remember the presence that grunted in my ear: "I'm gonna get you." I shudder. Maybe Cindy was just being nice. Maybe God really is punishing my family.

I know God isn't a bad God, but he does have righteous anger. Jacob says it's because God is holy, and if he didn't hate sin he wouldn't be true to his character. God *had* to strike down all those bad people in the Old Testament because if he didn't, he wouldn't be God. God ordains everything. He knows the number of hairs on our heads and he directs our paths and he knows the future. He must have not only known this was going to happen, but he must have wanted it to happen. The thought stings.

I relay my conversation with Cindy to Eleanor when she calls.

"This is bullshit," she says. I've never heard her say that word before, and it came out so powerful and real and more healing than all the Scripture other people recited me.

"It is. It is bullshit," I say, bouncing the word back. "But everything happens for a reason, right? So there must be a reason for this."

"Shut up," she says. "Did your pastor's wife tell you to say that?" I let out a shocked laugh. "Come to Washington and visit me. Get out of there. You don't need to hear about generational sin right now."

"I can't. I start college in ten days," I say.

"Wait, you're still going?" she asks.

"Yeah. I need to get back on the horse," I say. I don't really know what that means, but I heard someone else say it.

"Then come before you start school," she says.

"The church is doing some nice things for us that I want to be here for," I say.

"Like telling you God hates you?" she says.

"No," I say. I feel defensive. "Like money drives and stuff. And the Trackside Tavern is doing a benefit concert in our name. Cindy is taking me shopping next week for college clothes."

"Well, that's good I guess," Eleanor says.

"And people are donating a lot of stuff," I say.

"Like what?" she says.

"Some good stuff, like stuff we need. Some of it is really nice," I say.

"And some of it is . . . shitty?" she says.

I laugh. "Yeah. Like old mattresses and broken furniture. It's weird. I guess we're supposed to be grateful," I say.

"Oh yes, because you're *fire victims*," she says. "I'm thinking of sending you some used dirty socks that won't fit you. What is the address of the place you're staying? You're welcome."

Eleanor makes me laugh somehow in the midst of all this, and not because I feel I have to be cheerful around her, like I do around everyone else. I'm tired of people saying "I can't comprehend how you must feel," and then quoting a scripture God gave them to share with me.

The thing is, I can't comprehend it either. All I know is it was a hot day, a dry summer, a forested canyon, and there was one spark from a propane stove, and now I'm talking about God's punishment and old mattresses with Eleanor. I can't comprehend how something as tiny as a spark from a stranger can lead to something so big, so life altering, so permanent.

I'm not angry with God. I know that worse things happen to people around the world every day. Who am I to shake my fist at God over losing some *stuff*?

I am angry with myself for thinking my faith was special or somehow different from everyone else. I wonder why someone would spend so many exhausting years earning God's favor if when the moment arises—a moment that begins with a single spark—the flames will destroy everything anyway.

I spread my red-and-black Mickey Mouse comforter on the top bunk in my new dorm room. When Mom and I found it at a thrift store a few days ago, complete with matching sheets and pillowcases, we were so excited. At the time, it felt like a promise that I'd be okay going to college in just a few days.

Now I'm not so sure. The comforter looks worn and kitschy next to my new roommate's teal bed-set straight from the Pottery Barn bag. My meager belongings look embarrassing next to her things.

I'm enrolled in the Pentecostal college that hosted the Missionettes camp I went to years ago. It's a pretty campus, nestled in the redwoods and close to the ocean. I've not been assigned to the exact dorm room I slept in during that camp, but I am just across the hall. The coincidence doesn't tickle me the way I thought it would. I've spent the last week in a blur of tears coming from raw and itchy eyes. My heart doesn't stop pounding, even when I sleep.

My roommate, Whitney, is still having boxes of things carried in by a trio of cute boys. She orders them around and they listen and smile, seemingly grateful to be in her presence.

"Boys are so silly," she says to me when they leave to get another load from her car.

"Yeah they are."

"So when is the rest of your stuff coming?" she asks. The fruit of my shopping trip with Cindy takes up a small corner of our shared closet.

"Oh. This is it," I say. "I don't really have a lot of stuff right now. Weird timing, but my family's house burnt down a week ago."

"Are you serious? That is *awful*. You poor thing," she says. She gives me a hug. The physical contact feels nice. I've been wondering what I'm doing here since I watched my parents drive away an hour ago. I wanted to chase after them, but that's what someone weak would do. I will go to college. I will push on.

"Yeah. But at least my dad saved the animals," I say, tearing up.

"Hey, so until you get more clothes, would you mind if I took up your side of the closet? I kind of have a fashion fetish," she says.

"Sure, yeah, that's fine," I say. I guess there's nothing wrong with her asking me. May as well use the space. Why do I resent her, though? She smiles and takes a hunk of dresses still on their hangers and puts them on my side of the closet.

"Let me know if you want to borrow anything," she says.

"I don't think I'll fit into your stuff," I say. Whitney is tiny with a mousey little voice, and I already feel like a Komodo dragon next to her.

"Well, maybe some accessories then," she says. She smiles.

"College is the best time in your life," I read in a Christian teen magazine last week. I can't let a silly forest fire get in the way. I can't let this ache in my heart stop me from thriving in college. That's what Satan would want me to do.

"Hey, so tonight, do you want to go to downtown Santa Cruz?" she asks.

"Sure, that would be fun," I say.

"Wear this," she says, throwing a slinky teal blouse at me. "It's big on me."

Whitney drives us to Pacific Avenue, the vibrant hub of beach town Santa Cruz. I roam in and out of bookstores and gift shops thick with the smell of incense. A man with dreadlocks to his mid-back and a pierced eyebrow whizzes by us on a unicycle. A couple women in long black skirts huddle on the sidewalk with their guitars and their pit bulls.

We walk by a *tapas* restaurant. Neither of us knows what *tapas* are, but we hear lively Latin music pulsing from its second floor, so we wander in and make our way upstairs to see what's going on.

It's a dark dance floor, packed with bodies. Outside the air is crisp and cool, but in here, it's warm like church on a summer night. I watch couples twirl each other around and bend their bodies in fluid movements, so intuitive and free, like a wild rushing river. I'm mesmerized. Whitney is whisked away by a man to dance. She looks back at me and shrugs with a smile. I give her the A-OK sign, and figure I'll watch her for one dance and then we'll leave.

As I'm waiting, a man approaches me. I'm taller than him, I notice right away. He bows and takes my hand.

"I've, uh, never done this before," I say.

"It's okay. It comes natural," he says.

I step on his feet a dozen times in the first few minutes of the song. He smiles each time.

"I'm sorry."

"It's okay. You're stiff. Relax. Move your hips," he says.

Move my hips?!

I remember Candace warning me against moving my hips years ago. *When we make things about our body, we distract people from Jesus.* But Candace isn't here, is she? Neither is Jessa, nor Jacob, nor

Danny, nor any of the people who would tell me this is wrong. So I jut my hip to the right, and then to the left and feel my body loosen with each move. I feel the music move through my body in beats of three, one-two-three, one-two-three. My dance partner smiles at me approvingly and lifts his hand. Instinctively, impulsively, I twirl around, keeping in the beat. I feel Whitney's silky top rubbing on my torso as I move. I feel my heart pounding, not because I'm worried about anything but because I'm out of breath from dancing. I feel light for the first time since the fire.

The song ends, and I curtsey for my dance partner, but I really want to kiss his small feet and thank him for setting me free. I dance with a dozen more partners, stepping on their feet sometimes, and laughing and twirling and moving my hips on the one-two-three. Maybe I'll be okay after all.

I'm lying in my bunk bed later that night, writing in my prayer journal when the guilt smacks me hard.

I have this pressing sense I grieved the Holy Spirit on the dance floor, but I can't put my finger on how. Was it the shiny top, or the moving of my hips, or this fuzzy new awareness of my body? I don't know. I tell God everything, and I promise him I won't go salsa dancing again.

The lightness I felt earlier tonight now sinks in my heart like a lead fishing weight. My eyes are stinging again, my heart is pounding again, and I'm angry and I can't explain why.

By midsemester, I'm done trying to get back on the horse. I show up to my classes in a trance and then stop by the cafeteria to get dinner to go so I can eat on my bed and watch YouTube clips of the house burning. I know I am supposed to move on from my grief, but I don't know how. I think I need to pray more. I think I need to press in to God. But my feet have no traction, and every step I take I am slipping away.

Whitney is having the college experience I thought I would have. She has amassed a group of fun girlfriends and tall boys who want to date her. She leads worship in chapel and takes trips to the beach on weekends. She no longer invites me to do things with her, and she doesn't even like to be seen walking to the cafeteria with me. She walks ahead of me with her friends, even if we leave at the same time from our room. At least she still lets me use her hair straightener and shows me how to do it right. It's pretty clear she wants to make me more presentable on campus for her sake, but I don't care. I like how sleek my hair feels when it's straightened, and I try to do it on the days I don't roll out of bed four minutes before class.

I'm lying in bed with my eyes closed, thinking of all these things, while Whitney is using our dorm phone to talk to one of the boys who wants to date her. I'm not really listening.

"That's pretty gross, but your roommate can't possibly be weirder than mine," she says in a hushed voice. She must think I'm asleep. I hold still and listen. "All she ever does is cry, and her shoes are *so ugly*. I shouldn't be so mean. I think they were given to her because she's poor." I stare at the ceiling, mortified and trying not to move as I cry. *I need to go buy my own straightener*, I think. And I need to get out of here.

The next day, I phone my grandma to tell her what a great time I am having in college. She knows I am lying, like I had hoped she would, and she drives up with two of my cousins for a marathon of ice cream outings, back tickling, and beachcombing. We stay at my uncle's house in Santa Cruz, and for a few days I'm happier than I've been in months.

As we say goodbye in the college parking lot, Grandma reaches in the trunk of her car and pulls out a box. It's full of classic Disney movies on VHS, my favorites from my childhood—*Snow White and the Seven Dwarfs, Bambi, The Little Mermaid,* and a dozen more.

"I know this is a hard time for you. You don't have to pretend it's not," she says. She hands me the box. "I hope these movies remind you of happier times."

We all hug goodbye and I lug my movies into my room. I have a ten-inch screen TV with a built-in VHS player that was donated to me anonymously. I stick *Snow White* in and make a fort out of blankets and pillows on the floor. When *Snow White* is over, I watch *Aladdin,* and then *The Jungle Book.* I'm whisked away to a time before. A time before the revivals, before the fire, before the fog. I hide for days in the fantasy of enchanted forests and fairy dust and singing fish while my peers go to prayer meetings and couple off. By October, all the other girls in my dorm wing have boyfriends, or at least "intentional friendships" with boys, whatever that means. I am so lonely, and I don't even know if I care. I have stopped trying to read the Bible. None of it makes sense anymore, and the text is always blurry.

I call Jessa.

"God feels so far away," I say.

"Have you been pressing in and keeping up your prayer life?" she asks.

"Not really. I mean, I do pray sometimes, but it feels so forced. I want it to flow from me like it used to."

"Why don't you pray out loud with me right now?" she says.

"Maybe later. I have to go right now." I hang up. I turn on *Beauty and the Beast.*

On the night of the campus's big prayer event, I force myself to throw on a sweatshirt and leave my dorm to attend. The chapel is packed. The speaker opens the floor to anyone who has a word to share. I raise my hand. I walk forward to the front of the chapel stage, ready to deliver a prophecy for the hungry crowd. I feel more powerful with each step. I can do this. I look out my audience and see the desperation in their eyes. They are waiting for me to speak something into their lives, hoping I will say something they can cling to and believe in, something that will make them cry cathartic tears.

I press the microphone to my lips and begin.

"I feel the Lord is pressing me to tell this room that no matter what we've been through, God has a plan for us," I say. The crowd cheers and I hear "amens" around the room. "And I feel in this moment that God's plan for us is to move mightily on campus this year," I say. I close my eyes. "Mightily like the hand he used to defeat his enemies thousands of years ago," I say. More cheers. My hands are shaking.

"Yes Lord!" someone shouts from the back.

"Mightily like the force of a river, constant, rushing over us, carrying us despite our brokenness!"

My teeth are clicking into the microphone, but I continue.

"I hear the whispers from the Holy Spirit saying, 'This is our season of restoration! God will bring beauty for ashes, strength for pain, gladness for mourning.' Say it with me, *Yes, Lord!*"

"*Yes, Lord!*" the room chants back at me.

"This is our time, people! This is our time," I say. I stand in silence on stage, basking in the moment. People are cheering and crying and raising their hands in worship.

I hand the microphone to the speaker and step down. I walk down the aisle, to the back of the chapel, and outside. I walk past my dorm room and into the woods behind campus, where the only lights are the stars and the only noise is a chorus of crickets. I sit down and lean against a redwood tree and shiver. Santa Cruz evenings are colder than I'd thought they'd be. I sit there, breathing in the chilly air and breathing out steam. I listen to the crickets long enough that I begin to hear them chant: *You're a fraud. You're a fraud. You're a fraud.*

I didn't have a prophecy, not one bit. I made it all up. Why I did it, I can't even say, but I think I wanted to hear people say "Amen" to something I said. I think I wanted to prove something to them. I think I did it because I want to be loved.

Eleven

I don't return to college in the spring. I finished the fall semester thinking I would, but also somehow knowing I wouldn't. Two days after Christmas, I drove to the campus one last time to gather my belongings and sign exit forms, feeling not defeat but hope. I was going back to the place I belonged. I wanted to revive the late nights at the park and the powerful prayers, the afternoons at Jessa's. I thought I could leave the fog behind.

I wanted to be in Pine Canyon again, so that everything would be okay.

I'm still feeling hopeful as I get ready for church this Sunday morning. I spread cream cheese on my bagel, pull on a polyester dress, and head out the door as usual. On the drive, I roll down the window and stick one hand out, letting it lift and dive in the wind as I zip down the windy mountain roads. I pass the abandoned orchard where I used to pick ripe pears in the fall, and the meadow where, during one of my adventures with Jane and her mom, Ilene, we found a pile of bones we imagined to be a human skeleton. Jane's mom took the bones to the police and the veterinarian and the town doctor, and they all said they were deer bones. Jane's mom wouldn't have it and to this day is convinced we found a dead body that day. I pass the flock of peacocks that are always sunning themselves in the road on early mornings. They are owned by an old friend we call Peacock Bill, a gold miner with a long gray beard. Dad says Peacock Bill isn't allergic to poison oak, and takes a bottle of Ranch dressing to the river with him to eat poison oak salads. Or maybe that is someone else Dad knows. Anyway, I'm skeptical. I think about the year Peacock Bill gave me one hundred dollars for my birthday. I'm pretty sure I made him a thank you card with a peacock on it. I haven't seen him in years.

Once in town, I pass the little market where Dad and I used to wait for the train with our Squeezits and Dr. Peppers. I turn left on Grove Street past the post office without turning on my blinker, as usual. As I pull closer to the church, I can make out the crowd surrounding the concrete ledge. Jessa, Dahlia, Heather, Mark, Kevin are all there. I park in the spot I always do, parallel on the street in front of one of the neighboring houses. I turn off my engine. I can hear laughter and music. The worship team must be warming up. Clutching my keys, I pause. I wonder what would happen if I stay here a bit longer. Aware of the moment's power, I stay in my car. The group of people outside migrates inside after a while, and still I sit in my car. I can hear worship starting up. Pastor Frank's voice carries out to the street. No wonder the neighbors complain. It is time to go in now. But I don't.

It started last Sunday with Pastor Frank jumping around the pulpit, exuberantly talking about the upcoming elections.

"Let's get on our knees to elect a man who gets down on his!" he shouted. People were dancing up and down the aisles with flags.

"Jesus, let freedom reign! Let freedom reign!" Cindy said from behind the piano.

"Beautiful, Cindy. Let's sing it together. Everybody raise your hands and sing 'God Bless America' with me!" Pastor Frank said.

Everybody raised their hands—except for one man who is dating one of the college-age girls who grew up in the church. This was his third or fourth time visiting, and he seemed a little more reserved than the average Pine Canyon Assemblies of God attendee. Pastor Frank honed his stare at the one pair of hands that wasn't in the air.

"Excuse me sir, do you have a problem with raising your hands to the Lord?" Pastor Frank asked.

"No," the man said.

"Then why don't you do it now?" Pastor Frank said, leaning in close.

"I'm not really feeling led to right now," the man said.

"If your leader is leading you, then you are *led,*" Pastor Frank said.

The man looked at his girlfriend, who was staring at the floor, and then back at Pastor Frank, and then around to the rest of the congregation. He lifted his hands, but only a few inches. Pastor Frank kept staring at him with narrow eyes and then stepped away.

"Now, let's try that again, Church. Let's lift up our voices to the Lord!" he said. We sang together, our hands in the air. The blood left my fingers, and then my hands. Our voices blended together as one.

I can't shake Pastor Frank's face from last Sunday, his twisted lips and cold eyes. I put the keys in the ignition and turn it. I press my foot into the clutch and shift to reverse.

I drive to the park, run to the grass and lie on my back. I don't realize until I get here that this is where I intended to go all along. Except for a pair of squirrels chasing each other up and down the buckeye tree, I am alone. I pull out the journal from my purse, and instead of taking notes from Pastor Frank's sermon, I write until my wrist aches. I look up at the cloudless sky and pray myself into a peaceful sleep. When I wake, I dig out my cell phone from my bag and check the time. It's noon. Pastor Frank is likely still in the middle

of his sermon with another hour to go. I stretch my arms behind my
back and thank God I'm not there.

I've loaded up on classes at the community college, because while I
have no idea where I want to end up, I know I want to have a degree.
In February, after six months of living in a friend's cabin off the grid,
my parents haul a doublewide modular home to their property, on
the spot where the old house stood. My brother and I pick bedrooms,
and I hang an embroidered tulle canopy over my donated trundle
bed. It is the closest thing to home I have felt since August.

Something has changed at youth group since I've been gone.
Jacob and Jessa are now always giving us stern looks whenever somebody says the word *heck* or because someone pierced something
other than their earlobes, or because we are flirting with each other
too much. We don't talk about it, but I can tell my brother has had
enough. He is starting to do things purposely to rile Jacob and Jessa,
like making fun of Christian bands in front of them. A few of the
other kids have started smoking cigarettes behind the church building. Heather came back from college for spring break with dreadlocks
and told everyone she wasn't a *fundamentalist* anymore, whatever
that means. People are backsliding all over the place.

Also, there's a new girl at church, and she and Dahlia are best
friends now. The girl's name is Leah, and she comes from this strict
homeschooled family with eleven kids. She's not even allowed to
cut her hair or wear makeup, and Jessa thinks she's just the godliest
thing to walk the earth since Christ himself. I want to go back to my
role at church—Dahlia's best friend, Jessa's favorite—but I seem to
have been replaced. Leah doesn't seem to enjoy having me around
either, and lucky for her I'm not there all that much. I'm busy with my

college classes and my new job as a private tutor. I don't do as much
with the youth group as I used to.

Meanwhile, Pastor Frank, Cindy, Jessa, and Jacob are planning to
host a secretive youth retreat to clamp down on some of the budding
relationships and flirtations they are seeing unfold in us teens. They
call it the "Relationship Retreat." Paul and I call it the "Reckoning
Retreat." We know we are going to get lectured, but we go anyway.

On the night of Reckoning Retreat, we girls stay over at Frank
and Cindy's, and the boys are at the property where we used to rake
leaves. We watch video sermons about modesty and purity, and then
eat popcorn and watch *Father of the Bride*, but fast-forward the part
where the father tells his daughter and her fiancé to use a condom.

After the movie, Jessa goes upstairs and leaves us to sleep on the
floor. We unroll our sleeping bags, thinking we are alone, and begin
to whisper in the raw, revealing tone girls reserve for late nights and
slumber parties. Dahlia talks about a new boy she likes, and I say she
should perfect a sultry dance to lure him in. Leah giggles.

"Yeah, Dahlia, you should do the Macarena in the middle of
church! That should get him," Leah says.

We all laugh. I wonder if maybe Leah and I can be friends after
all.

"Girls," a voice from upstairs says. It's Jessa. I didn't think she
could hear us from here. "Your conversation hurts my heart. After
all we learned today? Jesus is so grieved by this," she says. We look at
each other with big eyes, trying not to laugh. "Jesus, wash over these
girls and correct any un-right spirit in them tonight," she starts to
pray out loud without any announcement. We can't see her, but her
voice hovers over us like the voice of God.

The prayer goes on for a long time, but I'm not listening. For the
first time, I realize Jessa doesn't know how to have fun.

Jessa seems to be getting stranger lately, and her strangeness is only compounded when a week or so after the purity retreat she announces she is pregnant with what she knows is a boy, despite not having an ultrasound. This is no ordinary pregnancy to an ordinary boy, of course. This boy has a calling, an anointing, and a secret name blessed by Pastor Frank. This boy is going to do great things for God, and all of us have the privilege of knowing him. For weeks, worship services are dedicated to this baby, and the whole church is obsessed with him, even though his due date is months away.

I am going along with the hoopla, but I'm starting to think it is all a little much. The baby's secret name especially bothers me, the way Jessa and Jacob whisper it in each other's ears when I am standing right there, and the way they give the youth group clues about it. It starts with a "J" and is found in the Bible, they say, as if we care enough to make a biblical scavenger hunt out of it. Jeremiah? Josiah? Jedediah? I can't be bothered.

Jessa quit her job at Starbucks shortly after she found out she was pregnant to dedicate herself to full-time nesting. My invitations to her house for pasta and mentoring conversations are growing sparse, and when we do meet, she spends most of the time talking about the prophetic baby growing inside her.

"It's like she thinks she's giving birth to the Messiah," I tell Dahlia after youth group one night.

"Or, like, a minor Old Testament prophet at the least," she says.

"Annoying. Why can't it be just a regular baby like everyone else's?"

"Because this baby has a 'spiritual legacy,'" she says, mimicking Pastor Frank's baritone voice.

I know we are being mean, and I want to be excited for Jessa like everyone else. But I am not excited. I am seething, and scared of losing Jessa. I am feeling regretful about that conversation with Dahlia when a month or so later, I am sitting in Jessa's car, her belly grazing the steering wheel, her whole body frowning. She invited me to do errands with her, which I jumped at, since we haven't spent time together in weeks. We are on our way back to church for youth group when she pulls to the shoulder outside the Catholic Church on Main Street. She yanks up the parking brake. I'm not sure why we are here.

"There's a lot of drama at youth group right now, which I'm pretty sure you know about," she says.

"I'm pretty busy with my college classes to really know."

"Oh, I think you do, though," she says.

I am beginning to feel like Jessa has planned this talk the whole time, and saved it for last, that this is the reason she called me to hang out today.

"There's people I get along with better than others, I guess." My nerves pulsed to my fingertips.

"I think it's more than that." Her voice is picking up and her face is red. "I think it's really ugly stuff in the spiritual realm. I don't know what happened to our perfect youth group." She looks like she is about to cry. "I don't know what I should do. Am I going to need to stop going to youth group?" she says.

"Why would you do that? We love you," I say.

"I just can't have my baby exposed to all this toxic stuff," she says, patting her belly.

I stare out the window and watch people enter the church for afternoon Mass.

"It's my job to protect my son, and I'm afraid taking him to youth group could tarnish his anointing." Her voice is getting louder, a little like her dad's.

"Are you saying you're going to quit?"

"I just can't expose him anymore," she says. "I think you know what I'm talking about."

I feel guilty, but for what I'm not sure.

"But he's not even born yet," I say.

"Well, yes, but he could soak up the negative spiritual atmosphere. He's still a person, even if he is in my belly. And I am his mother. My responsibility is to him."

Jessa has said some strange things before, but this is the weirdest thing I've heard anyone say ever. She turns to face me. Our noses are less than a foot apart, and I have a sudden urge to bolt out of the car and run away.

"I see some really unhealthy stuff between you and Dahlia."

"Really? She's my best friend at church. She's so much fun."

"I've known her since she was four years old, and I know she's a nice person. But I sense a dangerous spirit about her. Would you agree?"

"She's not perfect, but she loves Jesus."

"She doesn't talk to you about sexual stuff?"

"No, I mean, we talk about boys sometimes, but it's all pure."

"I'm not sure I believe that. I pray for that girl's fantasy thought life." Her voice cracks at the word *pray*. I sit up and turn my body away from Jessa, as far away as I can for sitting in the passenger seat of her car. "I think she looks at impure magazines at the grocery store checkout, and those sexual thoughts are dominating her mind."

"I wouldn't know about that."

"I'm married, and I don't even look at those kinds of magazines. And trust me, I don't need to. Jacob and I have a great sex life. A *great* sex life." She pauses, like she is thinking about having sex with Jacob right now. "I don't need to know all the tricks and positions in *Cosmopolitan* to please Jacob. Our relationship is deeper than that. If I don't need to look at that stuff, Dahlia certainly doesn't either. It is a dangerous fantasy to feed. I fear what she does alone at night," she says.

An acidic taste rises in my throat.

"Is it time to head over to the church yet?" I ask. Youth group has probably begun by now, and I feel the need to splash my face with water in the church bathroom.

"Watch who you're friends with," she says, starting up the car. "She has been rubbing off on you, and it's starting to show."

Kevin is at my parents' house when I get home from school. His normal uniform of a white Hanes shirt and khakis are black with char, and his arms have deep red gashes in them. He's been helping my dad clear brush leftover from the fire all day, and his eyes light up when I walk in the house. There is something heartbreaking about the way he sits on the couch, his crooked glasses coated with dust, so exhausted but summoning his last bits of energy to smile at me.

I'm weary too. I can hardly remember an existence where Kevin wasn't hovering in the foreground. I mumble a hello and go straight to my room to start my homework. I appreciate the help for my family, but this isn't Bible times. Jacob of the Old Testament worked in the fields to earn the favor of Rachel's father, but who cares? It isn't happening here.

Kevin knocks on my door. I shout, "Come in!" in a tone that really means *Go away.*

"Hi, er, I was wondering if you wanted to hang out this week," Kevin says, standing stiffly in my doorway and frowning.

"Sure, Kevin. I'll see you at youth group this week. Maybe we can all go to Starbucks after."

I have to treat Kevin this way because any kindness I show him fuels his obsession. I've known Kevin has liked me ever since he gave me that journal two years ago, looking at me all meaningfully one night after youth group. It wasn't until after I got the journal home that I noticed he'd written a note to me in the inside flap in his perfectly proportioned geometric caps. I'd tossed the journal under my bed and wished the gift had come from someone cute.

Dahlia and the other girls tease me about him, because they think Kevin is gross, but I don't think there is anything gross or funny about the situation. I think it's kind of sad. Sure, he is older than me and a little strange, but I feel sorry for him. I mean, I am dying for a boyfriend, but even I will never consider dating Kevin. Despite how hard he tries, Kevin is unappealing based on his looks and personality, two things he cannot change.

"Er, yeah, that will be fun, but I, uh, was hoping to hang out with just you for a little bit. I need to tell you something," he says.

"Okay. What's up?"

"No. I'm not ready to tell you now," he says.

I roll my eyes. *Gosh, Kevin, get yourself together.*

"Then . . . how about Wednesday? After class I'll meet you in the church parking lot. Four o'clock," I say.

"Yeah," he says. He is still standing, frozen.

"So I'll see you then," I say, waving him out of the doorway. "Bye."

On Wednesday, we are sitting in my car, parked outside the baseball diamond at the Pine Canyon Park where we used to come pray for revival. He had offered to drive, but I wanted control of this outing. I had no plan in mind, other than knowing I didn't want to get food or coffee with him. The less festive and date-like this encounter is, the better.

Kevin smells disgusting, like he's been dumpster diving. He is staring at his lap in the passenger seat of my car. My family is going to the movies in an hour, so I don't have long. I'm waiting for him to tell me he likes me, and then I will politely tell him I don't share his feelings, so I can get to the movies in time for the trailers. But Kevin isn't spitting it out.

"So you needed to tell me something?" I say, prompting him.

Long pause, again. I look over at him. He's gelled his hair, and he's wearing a polo shirt. Oh gosh, he dressed up for the occasion. I can hardly bear the thought of him squeezing gel into his comb as he got ready today, thinking of me. Then again, if he gussied up, he could have at least showered off the stink.

"Yeah," he says.

"Well, what is it?" I say. I want to say, *Look Kevin, this is never going to happen*, but I don't. These are words he needs to form. He gives me a desperate smile, and my heart aches for him. I had thought I wanted him to squirm today, to make him pay for all the obnoxious ways he's followed me around for years, but now that he's here, squirming, I want to comfort him. I realize the reason I'm here sitting with Kevin right now is because I care about him, and that I always have.

"Maybe, uh, this isn't the best time," he says. "But I've been telling myself that for years."

He lets out a huge sigh and closes his eyes. The sigh brings a wave of putrid, rotting death into the car, and I roll down my window trying not to let him see my disgust.

"Carly. The day I met you four years ago, I went home thinking, 'What a girl,'" he says. "But I knew I didn't deserve you. You are so beautiful and godly and free, and I . . . er, I am not. So I went to sleep feeling like I'd lost the love of my life." I look out the window, the strain in his voice almost too much for me to handle. "But then, that night, I had a dream. In it, you were covered with tattoos. From head to toe," he says.

"Okay," I say, feeling sick.

"The tattoos were a script in Hebrew, but in my dream, the Lord translated them for me. They said, 'Carly: Loving wife to Kevin.' They said, 'Carly: Loving mother of four.' They said, 'Carly: beloved by God,'" he says.

I was hoping for an I-like-you-will-you-go-out-with-me conversation in which I would reject him kindly, easily, and I could make my movie. But I guess if that were all he had to say, he would have said it years ago. This is something else entirely.

"The dream was so vivid I woke from it sweaty with an urgent sense to write everything down. God was so near me that night as I cried out to him. I said 'God, but she's too good for me,' and God said 'She is yours if you live your whole life for me,' and I wept," he says.

"Wow, that's . . . interesting," I say. I sound like an idiot.

"So from that day forward, I trusted God on his promise. I read my Bible every day and made him the center of my life. I felt if the promise was to come true, I had to believe that it would. I had to treat you like my future wife as an act of faith. There were times I knew it bugged you, that you wanted me to leave you alone, and it was hard for me to trust God in those times . . . especially when I saw how much you liked . . . Danny," he says, his voice choking on Danny's name.

"Let's not talk about Danny now," I say.

"So this is me, acting on that faith, and believing God even when it doesn't make sense," he says. My stomach turns upside down and I brace myself for what comes next. "Carly, will you prayerfully consider being my wife?" He says this without looking at me, without a ring, without a history that would make the question remotely sane.

His eyes are closed and he is heaving fast breaths as he waits for my answer.

"No," I say, turning to face him. "I am sorry, but . . . my answer is no."

"I knew it would be," Kevin says, and his tears start to fall into his lap. "I knew it would be. I fasted for three days for this, hoping for the promise to be fulfilled, but I always knew you'd say no."

Fasting. That's why he stinks so badly. His guts are crying out for food and he's denied them for three days. Because of a dream he had four years ago. Because of a word from God. The words of a thousand sermons come back to me. *Believe in the promises. Dwell in the Secret Place of the Lord and he will whisper revelations to you. Fast and pray for miracles. God has an incredible destiny for you.* But hearing them in practice now, with Kevin's heart smashed on the dashboard in front of us, their craziness comes into sharp focus. This is insane.

"I'm sorry," I say again, but I'm not sure what I'm apologizing for. "Maybe God meant something else by that dream, do you think?"

"No. I know what God meant. He said we would be together, if—and only if—I lived for him. I fell short of that. I didn't live up to my end of the promise. And I'll have to live with it the rest of my life."

Believe in the promises. I can hear the Nazirite preacher saying it, his raspy voice filling the words with urgency and purpose. Or don't, I want to shout back at the preacher. *Don't believe the promises.* All these years, Kevin's been praying and believing and showering me with gifts because he believes in a promise, when all along there was nothing he could do to make me love him.

"Kevin, don't blame yourself. You could be the godliest man in the world and I still wouldn't—" I stop, realizing just how hurtful the end of that sentence would be to him. "And we still wouldn't be compatible." I hand him an In-n-Out napkin for a tissue. He wipes his cheeks and blows his nose.

"Without this dream, I don't know what I can believe in anymore," he says. I want to think he's being manipulative, but his words are too familiar. They take me back to the day one year ago when I reached out for Danny by the church fountain. *Carly, I'd like you to meet my girlfriend.* Before those eight words, believing came easy. Now it's a fight every day, and now in one word—*No*—I have done the same for Kevin. Believing will never be easy again.

"I know what you mean," I say, and he opens his eyes and looks at me.

"This dream got me through so much. Even when I knew it would never come true, even when every logical thing I knew about you and me told me it would never work, I clung to it."

I can restore his faith right now with a few simple words. I can prove that God exists and that he is good and that the promise Kevin believed isn't a lie. I can do that right now, for Kevin. Instead, I tell him we can still be friends, feeling like a stupid cliché. The words are genuine, but so empty and small, so not enough for what he needs right now. Knowing this, I don't try to fill the void with more empty words.

I start my car.

He doesn't speak on the short drive back to the church. I pull up by his car, and he gets out and looks at me with lost eyes, and I know he is saying goodbye. "Eat something," I tell him, but he doesn't answer. He walks to his Thunderbird without turning back.

Twelve

"Are you doing okay, Carly?" Cindy asks. She tilts her head at me like a concerned parent.

This is my second mission trip to Juarez, and because of what happened with the demons last time, we are staying at a hotel on the El Paso side. We've spent the day painting a food bank and telling Bible stories to children. I was hoping to dip in the pool with Dahlia before retiring for the night, but Cindy had said she wanted to speak with me privately, so I followed her into the hotel lobby, where she led me to one of those stiff couches that are mostly for decoration. Now Cindy is looking at me with these serious eyes, and I'm really wishing I were in the pool with the rest of the kids. But Cindy's been so good to me this trip. She held me as I vomited next to her on the plane, and later, she took care of me when I started my period minutes before taking the stage for the drama we were to perform for a Mexican church. With all the poise of a matriarch, she wordlessly motioned for Dahlia to take my role in the drama and led me away. She washed my long, flowing skirt under the water from the pump house, telling me not to worry about a thing, that nobody noticed. I owe her at least this.

"Yeah, I'm doing fine," I say. "I really feel God here this week."

She raises her eyebrows as if she doesn't believe me. "I really sense that you're not okay."

"Really?"

"I don't want your precious heart to backslide," she says. Her voice is sing-songy and sweet, almost like she is tucking a baby in its crib. I pause to take in what she's saying. I feel hurt and defensive. But if I am defensive, maybe that means she is right. It has been a rough year, and I don't have the fire I used to have, and there are all these doubts and sad feelings floating around in my mind, and I don't know how to deal with them. I cry almost every day, and I don't even know why I'm crying. I feel alone and scared.

"I guess I have been struggling now that you mention it."

"Do you think it's because you are drifting from Jesus?" she asks. "It's my responsibility to keep you living for the Lord. Something is changing in you and we can all see it."

"You mean you've talked about this with other people?"

"Honey, it's so obvious. It's written all over you."

I marinate in silence for some time, basking in this meaningful, maybe even powerful, moment. Cindy understands me. She sees my pain and she wants to help. I should have gone to Cindy with my fears long ago; she knows me so well.

I lock eyes with her, so she can read my soul and see my confusion and pain and hold me until it goes away, like she did when I got sick on the plane. She stares right back like she is reading my heart, just like the preacher did so long ago. The silence and the eye contact continue, but I'm not uncomfortable. We don't need to use words. Everything is being said right now, from my dark, stone-blue eyes to her bright, sky-blue eyes. The ache in my heart opens up and begins to trickle away in this moment, in something so simple as a look.

Cindy clears her throat. "Why are you staring at me with lizard eyes?" she says.

Startled, I scoot away from her. I feel like I've been slapped. She wasn't reading my heart at all. She was thinking about my ugly eyes. My thoughts are racing again; I'm gripped by a memory of being eight years old and posing for a soccer team photo. We had to retake the picture because the photographer said I was staring into the camera with "lizard eyes." Everyone laughed.

It is the exact phrase, used ten years later, and I'd laugh at the coincidence if I weren't doing everything I could to stop from breaking down.

"Well?" she asks, and I realize she actually wants an answer.

"I was . . . just thinking," I say, straightening up and folding my arms.

"Well it seems like you have a lot to think about—or something. I'll leave you here to do that," she says. "I'm tired and I need to have some prayer time before bed. Pray about what I said tonight." She gets up without looking at me and walks away. I hear the elevator ding, and the doors close on her.

I sit on the stiff couch in the lobby for an hour, alone, stunned. The concierge brings me a bottle of water and a handful of after-dinner mints and asks me if I'm okay. I nod and thank him for the water.

I am drifting away, Cindy is right. I am drifting away and I can't stop. The things I used to do to ground myself—the prayer, the Bible reading, the mission trips, the worship—aren't working anymore, and I am floating away like a girl with all her gravity taken away from her.

As the summer continues, I find myself going to youth group out of obligation. But still I go, because it's what I know to do. I stop arriving early to hang out, and sometime am even late. One Thursday in midsummer I walk in five minutes late and people are playing Monkey in the Middle in the sanctuary with a pile of pale blue balloons leftover from Jessa's baby shower. Jacob leaves the game and flicks his neck in my direction, like one of those macho football coach greetings.

"Hi!" I say, and kick a balloon away from the Monkey. It takes me a second to register that his face is red.

"You. Come with me," Jacob says.

"Okay . . . Why?"

He doesn't answer. He leads me behind the stage up the narrow carpeted stairs toward the prayer room. The prayer room is tiny and rarely used because it's so cramped. I wonder why we are going to the prayer room right now. Maybe he wants me to pray with him over the service tonight. Whatever it is, he seems serious about it.

Jacob opens the door with a push. Jessa, my brother Paul, a parent volunteer, and Dahlia are sitting on folding chairs in a tight circle. Their knees are almost touching in the middle. I look at their faces and instantly know something is wrong. My brother is scowling and Dahlia is teary. The room is humid and smells faintly of mildew.

"Do you want to tell Carly why she's here?" Jacob says. I'm in trouble, I think. I'm in trouble for something big, and this is my intervention. This is my reckoning.

"She's here because this whole thing is stupid," Paul says.

Jacob stomps to my brother and stands over him. "Do not disrespect me, or I will throw you out of here."

"Do it," Paul says.

Jacob backs up to the middle of the circle and paces. I've seen Pastor Frank angry like this, but never Jacob. My brain is flipping through every church memory of the last few weeks for what we might be in trouble for and I come up with nothing.

"There is a Spirit of Negativity with you guys, and I've had it. I've had it. You hear me?"

"What's going on? Can someone please explain?" I ask.

"You know what's going on," Jacob says. Jessa pats the empty chair next to her and Jacob sits down. Jessa leans forward in her chair and looks at me.

"Carly, we need to intervene because you are backsliding," she says.

"You have a toxic spirit, and everyone can tell. Especially Leah. You have been cruel to Leah," Jacob says.

"Really? Is this because I didn't invite her to my birthday? You know I only invited like two close friends to that, and only one was from church?"

"Not just that," Jessa says. "You are bringing all kinds of bad spirits when you come through these doors." She pats her belly and I wonder if she thinks her son is being compromised right now.

Leah is not here, so I don't know how she feels about any of this. "Well, why doesn't she tell me this herself? I don't get it."

"It doesn't matter what you don't get," Jacob says, standing up again and getting his face close to mine. The whites of his eyes are giant, and dark blotches of sweat stain his shirt. "What matters is you have major sin in your life—all of you in this room—and until you confess, you are never coming out."

He sits back in his chair. There is a framed cross-stitch above him that says *Shalom*. I hear the sound of a balloon popping from downstairs, and then an explosion of laughter. If I close my eyes, I can picture myself downstairs with everyone else, having fun like the old days. It seems like just yesterday I was Jessa's favorite, and now I'm getting punished in the upper room.

Pastor Frank and Cindy went on a mission trip to Africa a couple weeks ago and left the church to Jacob and Jessa. Jacob had always been relaxed and childlike compared to Pastor Frank, but with the church left to him, he is earning new wrinkles fast.

The crease in his forehead is in full effect right now and it looks like it's deepening right in front of us.

I look at Jessa, hoping she will rescue me from this because I know, despite what happened a few weeks ago in her car, Jessa understands me. But her face is cold. I look at Dahlia, searching for one of those knowing looks we've swapped so many times before, but she looks straight ahead. I start to cry. I was stupid for coming back to Pine Canyon. I mean nothing to Jessa. I was miserable at college, but I'm miserable here too.

"You're making my sister cry. This is crap. I'm leaving," Paul says. He stands up and makes his way to the door, which makes me heave a deep sob.

"If you walk out, this is it," Jacob says.

"What is that supposed to mean?"

"You know what it means."

What does *it mean?* I think. But I don't want to know the answer. I can't handle any of this anymore.

"Jacob, let's calm down," the parent volunteer says. "You can't make him stay here." Jacob lets a long breath out and relaxes his shoulder a hint. Paul looks at me.

"Carly. Come with me," he says. "You need to get out of here." Through blurry tears, I look back at him. I want to get out of here. I want to so bad. But I don't even yet know why I am here, and Jacob and Jessa are angry with me, and I want them to love me again.

"No," I say. "I want to make things right."

"Things are never going to be 'right' here. It's messed up and it's never going to change. Come on, let's go."

"I can't."

"Please." He holds my gaze for another second, and I can see his heart breaking into pieces, and then I see him shutting it all down, shaking his head and turning his back to me, slamming the door on his way out. My anger surges and I stand up and punch the door. I broke my little brother's heart. And I'm stuck in this room with people who want to break me. I lean my head against the door for a moment, and then I fall back in my chair and hold my head in my hands.

"You have been straying from God for a while, but things are getting out of hand now," Jacob says.

"What *things*," I say between sobs. I can smell bitter sweat from my armpits. "I still don't know what you are talking about. Where is this coming from?"

I feel my phone vibrating from my back pocket. Jessa and Jacob watch me pull it out. They tell me not to answer. But it's Mom. I have to. Paul probably called her.

"Get out of there," she says, without saying hello.

"I can't."

"What do you mean you *can't?*"

"We are working things out," I say.

"I want you to leave that room and come home immediately," she says.

"You can't make me."

"This is really sick. This is really sickening. This is wrong."

"Mom, you don't understand."

"Get out of there." She is spitting out each word like they are hot coals.

I hang up. I want out of there more than she knows—Jacob is scaring me, and Jessa is in on it—but these are the people I trust with my life. They can't be wrong. If they *are* wrong, it has to be a misunderstanding that I can explain and we can all move on. We can laugh about it and go downstairs to play with balloons.

"I want to be godly and do what's right," I say. "So can you tell me how I can do better?"

"You have to change your heart. Both of you," Jessa says, glancing at Dahlia, who has been so quiet since I've been here, I almost forgot about her. Dahlia reaches over and strokes my hair. Her touch ignites another wave of sobs that had been building in my chest.

"I don't think I have a bad spirit. I really don't," I say.

"It's the Spirit of Rebellion," Jacob says. "A toxic spirit."

I quiver in my chair. I'm dizzy and so tired. My spirit cannot take in anything else tonight. I am spent. "Maybe it is," I say. My voice is papery thin and frail coming from my throat. "Maybe it is."

I drive home in a blur, my body spent from crying. My eyes feel like rubber and there are no tears left. *Everything was leading to this moment,* I think. Why didn't I see it coming? The purity retreat, the planned lectures and a voice from above, *Jesus is grieved by you.* Jessa patting her belly in her car, worried that her unborn son is absorbing my sin. Cindy and the concerned look, the lizard eyes. The rigid couch, the handful of mints sucked on alone. And now, this. This is what they've been working to. They've been planning for months to drag me and the people I love into that room to punish us. They had talked about the words they would use: *The Spirit of Rebellion. Backsliding. Toxic Spirit.* They had planned on beckoning us to go in that room and not letting us come out until they broke us.

They probably prayed together before bringing us up. They probably prayed that the Spirit would give them boldness and that we would be receptive to their words. I picture their heads bowed together, deep in prayer, feeling like the Spirit was on their side, knowing what was about to happen, and knowing I have no idea. Jessa saw my pleading look and ignored it. Jessa, who snores when she sleeps and makes salty pasta and has a permanent bruise on her left upper thigh. I know these things because I have shared beds and meals with her and watched her try on swimsuits and all those things mean nothing to me now, because the moment I needed her, she wasn't there. I no longer trust her. I no longer trust any of them.

I step into the modular home my family has lived in for several months now. Mom is on the couch waiting for me. Her arms are crossed and her eyes are dancing with rage.

"You are *brainwashed*," she says.

Not anymore, I think, but that's not what I say. I'm ready to fight. I'm ready to unleash the anger I've been holding down, toward Mom and toward the church.

"You don't know what you're talking about," I say, feeling it rise in my chest.

"Oh yeah? Then why didn't you get out of that room?"

"Mom, you don't know anything about this stuff." I feel the tears coming again. "Do you know how long I've had to pray against your generational sin just to stay alive? You are demonic. You are *demonic*." I don't even know what I'm saying, but the words keep coming out.

The angry flicker in Mom's eyes fades to cold, empty pupils. "Oh, now isn't that special. Well why don't you go live with your new family then?" She gets up and stomps around, looking for something.

"I don't want to go to them."

She pulls out her car keys from underneath a pile of papers with handwritten numbers on them. She's been working on getting the family's vital records replaced from the hospitals, social security, the state of California, and there is paperwork all over the house because of this.

"I'm *finished*," she says. She walks out of the house, slams the door, revs the engine of her car four times and drives away.

For three days, Mom and I mill around in the house together, not speaking, going to and from work or school in forced silence. Mom won't even look at me. I'm angry that my mother would withdraw from me when I've lost everyone else. I think so many times of calling Jessa—but I can't, or won't. I am done with Jessa. I am done with all of them.

I'm driving home from school in my new numb state, thinking about how I've lost it all, how silly I was to think I had lost everything the day the reality of Danny smacked me in the chest, or when I saw the pile of char on the news, and again with each step on that college campus, my roommate and her friends walking ten feet in front of me, realizing that college would not be the best time in my life. Now I realize all those losses were only preparing me for this one.

I feel my car spin out on the road just past the railroad tracks a mile from home. I slam on my brakes and come to rest beside a heaping roadside blackberry bush. I breathe in and out, holding the steering wheel tight. I'm alive, I think, and I let out a long breath.

I get out of the car and see that my driver's side front tire has blown out. I get out the jack and spare tire from the trunk and I bend over, wrangling the jack under the tire and trying to crank it up, but it keeps sliding from underneath the tire.

A car passes, and I recognize it just from its hum of her Honda engine. It's Mom coming home. I watch the car go by, and I kick the tire and put my head in my hands.

A few minutes later I hear a voice over me.

"Let's do this," Mom says, helping me up from the ground.

I hold the blown-out tire in place and try to lift as best as I can as Mom cranks the jack up. Together we pull off the tire, getting mud and oil all over our chests, and wrestle to attach the spare. We don't say much. "Lift now. You got it? Here, I'll pull on this side. Yeah, like that. There we go." These simple exchanges are the first we've had in days. Grease covers our hands. Mom and I will be okay. Maybe not right away, but we will.

As for people at church, I don't think so.

An envelope addressed to me comes in the mail with Jacob and Jessa's return address in the corner. It's been a few weeks and I haven't been to youth group since the night in the upper room. I open the envelope and find a typed letter in all caps:

DEAR CARLY,

WE PRAY ALL IS WELL FOR YOU AND YOUR FAMILY AS YOU APPROACH SUMMER THIS YEAR. WE UNDERSTAND THAT YOU ARE IN A CRITICAL TIME OF DECISION MAKING IN YOUR LIFE. YOU MIGHT BE WONDERING WHAT YOU ARE GOING TO DO FOR THE REST OF YOUR LIFE, OR MAYBE YOU HAVEN'T GIVE IT MUCH THOUGHT AT ALL. WITH THAT SAID, WE WANT TO TELL YOU WHERE JESUS IS DIRECTING US AS LEADERS AND WHERE YOU FIT INTO THAT DIRECTION.

SUMMER HAS NOW BEGUN AND JESUS HAS PUT A FEW TASKS BEFORE US THAT WILL REQUIRE A FAIR AMOUNT OF EFFORT TO ACCOMPLISH. AS WE TALKED AND PRAYED ABOUT OUR PLANS FOR THIS SUMMER, WE FELT VERY STRONGLY THAT IT IS TIME TO DO THE WORK OF MINISTRY. YOU ARE ONE OF EIGHT PERSONS WHO WE ARE ASKING TO PLEASE CONSIDER COMMITTING TO AN 8-WEEK INTERNSHIP THAT IS CALLED "EMBLAZONED SERVANT." THIS INTERNSHIP WILL TEACH YOU

TO BECOME A SERVANT OF JESUS AS YOU SERVE HIS PEOPLE AND THE PEOPLE OF OUR CITY.

PASTOR FRANK AND CINDY WILL BE OUR COVERING IN THIS MINISTRY, SO IT'S ALREADY A "GO." WE HAVE THE BLESSING OF THE FATHER OF THE HOUSE, AND THAT IS WHERE THE BLESSING OF JESUS CAN BE RELEASED OVER US TO DO THIS. SO PLEASE CONSIDER THIS THOUGHTFULLY. WE HAVE PRAYED OVER YOU AND BELIEVE THAT THIS IS GOD'S HEARTFELT DESIRE FOR THIS GROUP OF PEOPLE. IF YOU CHOOSE TO ACCEPT THIS INVITATION, MEET AT OUR HOUSE THIS MONDAY NIGHT AT 7 P.M. PLEASE DO NOT INVITE ANYONE TO THIS MEETING AND DO NOT SPEAK TO ANYONE ABOUT THIS. IT'S NOT THAT WE ARE BEING EXCLUSIVE, BUT WE HAVE SEEN YOUR LIFE AND YOUR COMMITMENT TO THE CHURCH, AND SINCE YOU ARE GRADUATED FROM HIGH SCHOOL AND CALL PINE CANYON ASSEMBLIES OF GOD YOUR CHURCH, WE WANTED TO OPEN THIS OPPORTUNITY TO YOU. IF YOU DECIDE TO COME MONDAY NIGHT, PLEASE COME READY TO COMMIT TO THE PURPOSES OF GOD ACCOMPLISHED FOR YOUR LIFE. WE WILL GIVE YOU ALL THE DETAILS IN PERSON. WE LOVE YOU AND WANT TO SEE GOD'S DESIRE FULFILLED IN AND THROUGH YOU.

IN CHRIST, JACOB AND JESSA.

I read it, and read it again. *They want me back*, I think. I show the letter to Mom, who shakes her head.

"It would be pretty hard for you to 'not speak to anyone about this' when your own brother didn't get invited," she says.

"Doesn't matter," I say. "I'm not doing it."

Thirteen

I woke up in the same teal tunic I'd worn the night before, its fabric now stretched and buckled around my twisted body, a patch of crusty vomit covering my belt. My mouth tasted bitter and dank. My eyes felt like they were tied to my brain by two giant rusty cables; I didn't dare look too quickly to the left or right.

"Good morning," my husband Joe said, bringing me a cup of coffee. I sat up on the air mattress we called a bed and brought the mug to my nose.

"So what happened last night?" he asked, his lips curving into a slight smile.

"Oh God," I moan. "They called me 'Jesus Girl.'"

"Jesus Girl?" His smile was more prominent now.

"Not funny. I got drunk and started talking about religion," I said. Joe looked serious, but like he was trying hard to stifle a laugh. He got up and started making toast. As he spread butter on thick pieces of wheat bread, I told him everything—the Long Islands, the fried chicken, the vision I had about Pastor Frank and pressed knees into stained carpet, how I broke my glass and fell on the floor, how the bouncer kicked me out. My left temple was pounding. I took off the sequined belt that cinched my gut, tossed it on the floor, and took a deep breath. I thought about what a fool I'd made of myself, what an idiot I must have looked like convulsing around on the floor (maybe not unlike the floor convulsions I used to partake in at the altar, I realized). But as I relived the events from the night before, I was shocked by the absence of something I'd come to rely on for years: shame. Without it, I felt light. And very odd.

"This is going to sound bizarre," I said. "But something happened last night, something I can't really explain. But I think I've been released."

Five years it took me to get from the Upper Room at Pine Canyon Assemblies of God Church to the floor of that bar in Boston. Five slow, confusing, hopeful, fast years. I wish I had a dramatic religious escape story, but the truth is my escape involved little choices each day that didn't seem like anything until they were strung together by days and weeks and months and years.

When I got that letter in the mail from Jessa and Jacob, I knew I had to find a way out of Pine Canyon. It was June, and too late to apply to most state colleges. I had heard about this new evangelical college near Sacramento in the newspaper, and I knew one girl from my community college statistics class was transferring there in the fall. On a mucky afternoon, I took a spontaneous trip by myself to this college and wandered around the flat, sparse campus, feeling heat radiate from the pavement. A man waved at me, and I pretended to not see him.

He approached me anyhow, and introduced himself as a resident director. He gave me a tour of the campus and told me it had been renovated from a defunct furniture warehouse. The buildings were postmodern in form with asymmetric, angled roofs and steel paneled walls. They almost felt otherworldly to me. The resident director led me to the financial aid office, a building smelling of fresh paper and Scotch tape. A smiling woman told me based on my grade point average, I could be eligible for a hefty scholarship if I applied soon.

Less than two months later, I moved into a mustard-yellow, stucco dorm building and began to learn about history and psychology in classrooms surrounded by brown fields and concrete. Although it was just thirty miles from Pine Canyon, I knew it was distant enough that I could slip away from my old church without ever giving a reason.

The week before I left for college, Pine Canyon Assemblies of God threw a party for all of the teens moving away. Jessa and Jacob took me aside that night and told me they loved me.

"You are so special just the way you are," Jessa said. "Never change." I hugged them goodbye, feeling guilty because I knew I would. But the change happened slowly. During my first semester at William Jessup University, I wrote a note to administration about the need for a dress code on campus. *The girls are so immodest,* I scribbled on my comment card at chapel. I left Pine Canyon Assemblies of God to escape the rules, but without them, I was lost.

Jessup had plenty of rules, to be sure. Highly regulated opposite-sex dorm visiting hours. No same-sex relationships allowed or any premarital sex whatsoever. No alcohol allowed for anyone involved in sports or student government. Any of these offenses could warrant being disciplined or kicked out. Still, compared to my old life, Jessup was uncharted territory.

Cindy offered to lead a Bible study for me and other Jessup students who were interested in learning more about "the Full Gospel," which meant speaking in tongues and the other Gifts of the Spirit that regular evangelicals don't practice. I never returned her phone call. When Jessa had her baby, I brought flowers to the hospital and visited for a few minutes. I stopped hearing from all of them after that.

A dress code was never implemented at Jessup, but as the weeks went on and my first semester passed, I stopped caring so much. By the end of my first year, I had bought a few spaghetti strap tank tops myself. My prayers during these months vacillated between desperation and apathy. I wrote out a verse from Revelation on a teal index card taped to my dorm room dresser:

"Nevertheless I have *this* against you, that you have left your first love. Remember therefore from where you have fallen."

I remembered Jacob preaching on this verse and talking about what happens if we let our hearts grow cold to the Spirit. Jacob used to say if we felt like we were drifting from God, close our eyes and think about a time we felt his presence and remember what it felt like. Remember how infatuated we felt, how alive we felt, how our souls were on fire. He said to return to that place in your heart.

I needed all the help remembering I could get. I got involved with a minority movement of Pentecostals at Jessup who spent a lot of time in the prayer chapel begging for the Spirit to move on campus. I joined them, because I thought they were my people. The regular evangelicals didn't accept me anyhow—in evangelicalism, Pentecostals are the cousin who shows up for Thanksgiving in a colorful wrap dress while everyone else is in Dockers and Polo shirts. They are accepted in the family, but begrudgingly. So I forced my way into these spirit-filled prayer meetings and prayed extra loud. I wanted the group to see I was proficient in being radical for Jesus. I said all the things I'd heard other preachers say that sounded good, like for the heavens to unlock supernatural powers on campus and for the Nazirite generation of students to arise. I was putting on a show, but sometimes it felt real. Occasionally, between my demonstrations of grandeur, I had quiet moments of feeling God beside me as I sat on the ragged couch in that prayer chapel, the lights dimmed and the harmonies of fellow students rising up around me.

"I'm back, Jesus," I whispered. "I'm back to my first love."

But these moments slipped away from me as soon as I left the prayer chapel. I couldn't hold on to them. I couldn't keep them. At the end of each prayer session, I felt deader than I had before. God didn't speak to me anymore. I felt permanently barred out from the Secret Place of God.

As my college years went on, I went to the prayer chapel less and less. I loved those moments of God beside me, but it felt like so much *work* to get there. The prayer meetings were long and tiring, and by going I was missing out on hanging out with the girls from my dorm. I liked those girls. They were funny and quirky and enjoyed filming parody movies, much like the ones my friends and I made with Dad's ten-pound Camcorder when I was a little girl. Once my new dorm friends and I borrowed a spoon from the cafeteria and a lighter from one of the boys and made a dramatic film about a heroin dealer. Another time, we put makeup and yarn on our chins and hung upside down from our bunk beds and filmed chin puppet movies. We laughed a lot.

I passed my old friends from the prayer chapel around campus and they nodded at me with heavy, concerned eyes like Cindy on the hotel couch. They didn't say anything, but they didn't need to. *We lost her,* I imagined them saying about me. *Another one backslidden.* I knew they were praying for my hardened heart at their meetings, because I used to do the same thing. It made me sad for them. The index card with the verse from Revelation tore on the edges and collected dust on my dresser until I finally threw it away. I wasn't so sure I was forsaking my first love after all.

In a way, I felt I was returning to it.

Joe wasn't anything like the man I pictured when I used to pray for my future husband. He never raised his hands in worship, and he sat in the back of chapel sessions at WJU, sometimes snoozing, exhausted after his 5 a.m. soccer workouts. He was quiet and reserved, and always dressed in the same pair of torn carpenter jeans, oblivious of how dorky he looked in them. Joe and I had crossed paths a few times in our college years, once in a ping-pong game in the student lounge area, and again at a mutual friend's birthday party.

The summer before my senior year, Mom and I were visiting in the living room of my rented house on a weekday afternoon. We heard a knock on the door, and I went to answer it. It was Joe, dressed in running shorts and holding a watermelon at his side.

"Alexis isn't here," I said, figuring he was here to hang out with my roommate.

"Actually, I stopped by to see you. Want some watermelon?" he said, inviting himself in and helping himself to a large knife and a cutting board from the kitchen.

"No thanks," I said. My on-again-off-again college boyfriend had recently said we were "done for good," and I had planned to spend the summer wallowing in my heartbreak. Watermelon was not in the plan.

"I'll just leave it here in case you want some later. Hey, want to go kick around a soccer ball with me?"

"No thanks," I said again, letting my irritation show. Soccer was not in the plan either.

"Okay, well I'll come by later!" he said, prancing out.

Mom looked at me and folded her arms. "Well, he seems nice. Who is he? You should go play soccer with him."

"That's Joe. He's just some guy my roommates know. And no, I don't want to. I'm hanging out with you today," I said. But I did watch him go out the door, noticing his sculpted calves and the bounce in his step.

Joe continued to come over that summer with watermelons and good cheer. He never charmed me with romantic speeches or his heart for God, but with the sheer steadfastness of his presence. When I got in a quarrel with a roommate, I found myself driving to his house to vent. He listened and made me a tuna sandwich with celery and crushed Ritz crackers. When I was sleepy on summer afternoons following my early morning shifts at Starbucks, he sat on the couch with me and watched movies. We snuck into hotel swimming pools on hot days. We talked for hours over frozen yogurt and Chinese food about our families, our travels, our favorite shows. We laughed a lot. He never swept me away, like I always pictured my future husband doing. It's just that I felt more natural with him around than without him around.

In the spaces between the lazy, contented summer days with Joe, I occasionally struggled with the loss of my fire for God. When school began in the fall, I tried to find a home at WJU's monthly student-led worship nights, called UPward, on campus. These weren't Pentecostal services by any means, but they were still emotional and long. I used to live for these kinds of events, a chance to sing and hear the voice of God. Now, I went out of guilt, out of fear. I went because I worried what might happen if I stopped.

"Want to go with me to UPward tonight?" I asked him. We were sitting in the backyard of my rental house, idling the afternoon away.

"No," Joe said calmly.

"No? What do you mean 'no'? Why wouldn't you want to go?"

"I just don't want to."

"Don't you care about worshipping God?"

"Sure, but I don't need to go to a worship night to do that."

"Um . . . okay, I guess I'll go alone," I said, hoping he'd change his mind when he heard my disappointment. I searched his face, but it didn't soften.

"Okay. Maybe we can watch a movie when you get back," he said.

"Maybe."

I drove to campus by myself, wondering if Joe wasn't right for me. Didn't I want a man who would push me into the things of the Lord?

The service had already begun when I arrived. Two tall pale guys with acoustic guitars and skinny jeans were leading the group in a song about touching Jesus, or Jesus touching us. Candles flickered around the stage, and the eyes of my fellow classmates were shut. I raised my hand and sang a harmony. I knew this song well.

When the song ended, and one of the worship leaders whispered a prayer into his microphone, I shifted my weight from one leg to another and dropped my hands to my waist. My mind wandered. I studied the worship leader's outfit. I wondered if I could convince Joe to wear skinny jeans instead of those ugly baggy jeans he loved. That could be a fun thing for us to do together—shopping. Almost like something a girl would do with her boyfriend. . . .

I caught myself in these thoughts and realized I was bored already.

I scanned the room. I didn't see any of my friends here—I saw people I passed on campus, people who I nodded at in the halls. I didn't know these people or their stories; these weren't the people I trusted, or the people who had been there for me in rough times in college. These weren't the people I shared meals with or tears with or long drives with. They were strangers. I watched them sway and utter secret prayers under their breath, and it was beautiful. I watched from the outskirts, but I didn't feel left out, or lonely or jealous at their relationship with God or each other.

When I turned to leave in the third song, it wasn't out of bitterness or anger. It was because I had found where I belonged.

I called Joe on my way home and asked him if he was still up for that movie. When I got home, my friends and roommates were making a human pyramid. "Join us!" they said. I jumped on the second level and my ninety-pound Romanian friend climbed to the top. Joe came through the door just in time to take our picture before we collapsed, laughing. One of my roommates made monkey bread, filling the house with a warm, sweet odor. We watched *Gladiator* and Joe and I sat closer than we'd ever had before, our arms touching. For the last hour of the film, our pinky fingers mingled under the blanket so no one else could see. I wondered at first if it was an accident on his part. I moved my hand away ever so slightly, and his pinky found mine again. We swapped timid smiles. And just like that, our friendship turned to romance, as natural and easy as it began.

A year later, we were done with college, engaged, and Joe was employed as a youth pastor at Northside Bible Church. Somewhere in the flurry of our romance, I had forgotten that Joe wanted to be a youth pastor. It was easy to forget, really. He never talked about it, and when he did, his eyes glazed over with boredom. He did not fit in with the other wannabe youth pastors at school who played guitar and talked about their heart for the Lord. I wondered if he had taken the job to please somebody else—because it didn't seem like it came from him. Regardless, I was about to be a youth pastor's wife.

On a fall Sunday, I was staring at the tile floor of the high school cafeteria Northside Bible Church met in, crossing my legs and wondering how I ended up here.

"I prayerfully urge each and every one of you to take one of these home with you," Pastor Chuck said, displaying a stack of blue and yellow political signs. "Put them in your windows, your front lawns, tape them to your cars."

I snickered. Somehow I doubted these church people would tape anything to their shiny SUVs.

"We as Christians must fight to protect the sanctity of traditional marriage!" Chuck said.

I closed my eyes and was taken back to another church seat, from another time. I saw Pastor Frank's jowls shaking as he paced the church, interceding for a particular candidate to be elected as president. There were voter ballots placed on every seat. I saw myself jumping up and down in heavenly agreement. *We will not stand for evil in our nation!* I was too young to vote.

Pastor Chuck wasn't a pacer or a screamer, at least from the pulpit. There would be no jumping or interceding in this cafeteria. But there would be a *prayerful urge* to take a sign.

Pastor Chuck kept talking about why Christians should support this political measure and then passed the proposition signs down the center aisle. When they made it to me, I looked to see who was watching me—knowing I was supposed to set a *Godly example*—and tucked one under my chair and passed the stack to my right. "We as Christians must fight," I muttered. I had spent my life fighting, and I was tired and beginning to wonder if I had been fighting for the wrong side. That afternoon, back at my suburban apartment, I taped the sign to the inside of my bedroom window.

I leaned against a wall and stretched out my legs, tape dispenser still in hand, and looked up at the back end of the sign. Rage welled up in me. *How dare he*, I thought. I thought of Pastor Frank, how he told me when to raise my hands. I stood up, ripped the sign from the window, stomped down the hallway, and stuffed it in the trash.

While in the kitchen, I found my roommate's vodka and poured some in a tumbler over ice. I sat on the couch, sipping my drink and letting it burn my throat as I waited for Joe to get home from his church staff meetings. The most I'd drunk before was a shot of Malibu rum in a Diet Coke with friends, and I had definitely never consumed alcohol by myself before. I laughed. The youth pastor's soon-to-be wife had thrown away her godly political sign and is celebrating by drinking liquor on the rocks. I could get Joe fired if they knew. If I was being honest, there was a lot that would get Joe fired if they knew. We were trying so hard to be pure but we could only go so many days without kissing on my twin bed. These charged make-out sessions seemed to happen once a week, on Sunday nights after he was home from his pastor meetings. The timing wasn't lost on either of us, although we didn't speak of it. He'd lie on top of me and whisper all the things he couldn't wait to do when we were married. Once when he house-sat for a church member, we spent the night together, fully dressed but wrapped up tight in each other's arms. After this, we began to do that more and more. We lived in the same apartment complex, and many nights we'd cuddle in his bed, me hiking one leg over his hips and placing my head on his chest. In his arms, I felt so peaceful I'd fall asleep within minutes. Then I'd awake at 2 a.m. and make the walk across the complex back to my own bed. Technically I hadn't spent the night.

No amount of spooning could get me as close to him as I wanted. No amount of kissing was enough. We held on to our ideals to not have sex, but we also knew that as a pastor and pastor's fiancée, we were pushing boundaries. We were always told that instead of asking if something is a sin, we were supposed to ask *how pure can we be?* It was a question we were both tired of asking.

My roommate came home and made herself a pot of coffee. She opened the trash to toss the grounds, and saw the sign.

"What's this sign doing there?" she asked.

"That douche-bag pastor made me take it home," I said.

"Want to talk about it?"

"Nope."

Before this, I thought Pastor Frank was an anomaly in the way he abused his power. I thought maybe it was the denomination—the Pentecostal way of idolizing leaders. Or I thought it was the demographics—the blue-collar, isolated town in the mountains that made it possible. But the same stuff was happening in this nondenominational, highly funded church plant on the wealthier side of a wealthy suburb. *It's everywhere*, I realized. In rich churches and poor churches, in hick towns and cosmopolitan cities, in Pentecostal churches and Catholic churches, in mega-churches and home churches. It's all the same. It's all about control. It's all about manipulation. I wanted nothing to do with it anymore.

When Joe was fired from the church that spring, I wasn't surprised. Pastor Chuck turned out to be a screamer too. He was livid at Joe because the youth group was growing with kids who hung out at the city recreation center, but not with the *right* kind of kids. Not with the kind of kids whose parents tithe.

Three weeks later, Joe and I said our vows during a June thunderstorm under two old-growth redwood trees and a string of white lights. Eleanor and Jane stood by my side. We were promising our lives to each other. We were making something new.

—

Boston is where we went to learn and unlearn. We chose Boston because of its wide selection of graduate universities, and because it was on the other side of the continent from our "Christian community" in California. Joe studied business and I studied journalism, because I finally admitted that all I ever wanted to do was write, and that I had buried that desire because I thought I needed to focus on winning souls. We settled into our apartment and navigated the city's public transportation, giddy to start our new life together. I was free from pretending. Or maybe I was free to pretend in new ways.

The first week of classes, on a quest to find a new posse, I invited a pale, quiet girl from my journalism research class to play trivia that night at a bar around the corner from campus. She declined, saying she had plans to Skype into her Life Group from her hometown church she was sad to leave behind. For a moment, I opened my mouth to have the "Oh, you're a Christian? Me too!" conversation with her, the conversation that at one time would have brought a hushed connection between us, the comfort and safety of knowing someone was in the same club as me. But I stopped. I didn't want to have that conversation anymore. I didn't want to be in her club.

Instead, I found a family in people who didn't have to know about my past, people who helped me forget. I threw myself into my studies with them, discussing pieces from the front page of the *Boston Globe*. We rode the train in the snow to the courthouse to get public records for assignments we tapped out on our laptops late into the night. We worked for eccentric professors and graded freshman essays to pay for our tuition. I didn't have to stand for righteousness, or speak the truth in love, or have all the answers, or live out some extraordinary calling. In my new life, I was a learner. I was a friend. It was simple.

One weekend night, Joe and I had our friends over, like we did most weekends. After our long days of study and work, we weren't usually up for hitting the town like some of the people in our program did. We chalked it up to *old age* since we were all creaky and decaying in our mid-twenties, but the truth was we just liked to sit and be with each other.

We turned on some Bob Dylan and uncorked a bottle of red wine and began to talk, and got into the rhythm of relaxing. We talked about our assignments, our professors, our families, teasing each other, taking in each other's young, beautiful faces. We were transplants to Boston, all of us living in a place foreign to us. I looked around the room. Home for Allie, Joe, and me was three thousand miles away, and that was the nearest of all the homes in the group of people sitting in our living room, who came from places like Norway and New Zealand and South Africa. All of us were making our home in each other.

None of them knew about the Jesus Days, as I called them. Sometimes I wondered what they might think of them. I pushed those thoughts aside. That part of my life was over. It was all behind me. There was no reason to talk about them now.

We laughed together, and laughed even more once the second bottle of wine was polished off. Then I made espresso shots for everyone with the coffee machine Paul got us for our wedding. The machine took up most the counter in our tiny kitchen. I served the shots in giant mugs and Mason jars and a Disneyland tumbler because it's what we had.

"Whipped cream anyone?" I said, squirting some in my coffee. We clinked our glasses together and sipped the coffee as the late night turned into an early morning.

"I'm just so glad we've found you guys," I said.

"I am too. You are our American family," Ingrid, a girl from Norway said. I could always count on Ingrid to say something sweet.

After we finished our coffees, our guests put on their shoes and coats and gloves to get home before the trains stopped. I hugged each of them goodbye.

When Joe shut the door after our last guest, we brought each other into to a long, quiet hug.

"I'm so happy. I'm so free," I said, my face pressed to his chest.

"Let's go to bed," he said.

Joe was snoring within minutes of lying down. I, on the other hand, had too much on my mind. What felt so right and easy with busyness and merriment around me felt heavy once I was alone. The old familiar anxiety smacked down on me like a bag of sand when I remembered what I was running from.

I wasn't really free at all.

"I'm backslidden," I said to the dark room.

A week later, I would declare this to my friends at a bar. I would say it, and I would fall from my stool and break my cup and flop on the floor until a bouncer kicked me out.

After the night at the bar, I began to talk. I began to tell stories for the first time, making sense of them as I went. I told Joe about my first experience with altar calls at Missionettes camp, how my heart pounded and how I felt like I couldn't breathe. It seems so obvious now—that was a panic attack, right? I told him what it meant to be a Nazirite, how it felt to speak in tongues; was it real or was I hypnotized? I recalled what it was like to be best friends with Jessa; if our friendship was true, then why do I feel dirty about it? I told him about Danny; was I delusional or did I get dumped? I asked these questions out loud, for myself. No answers came to my rescue, but I kept asking, asking, asking.

I told him about being touched on the bus in Romania. Had I

been sexually assaulted? "Yes. No question," he said, but I didn't need him to answer. As I remembered the story, I was hit with the guilt I felt when my leaders blamed me for wearing shorts, but as soon as the guilt hit my chest, it was replaced with a new, more robust emotion: anger. I pounded our pine IKEA table, and for the first time in years, I didn't feel shamed for it.

I felt *mad*.

As the winter snow began to melt away by late March, we began to take walks again. One Sunday morning, Joe and I were walking to a French bakery eight blocks from our apartment. I was recounting a story about a prophecy I received over my life, remembering it as I spoke. I'd been doing this a lot lately—remembering, retelling, making sense of it all.

"She was a preacher, wearing an Eddie Bauer puffer vest," I said. "I can't even remember how old I was, maybe sixteen or seventeen. It was at my church women's retreat in the mountains, in this little wooden chapel. Anyways, she said I was called to do great things." Joe nodded, so I kept talking. "She said there were two paths for me. One was a direct path, and the other was a meandering path. I could choose to take either of them, but the meandering path would be a painful journey," I said.

"And what was the direct path?" Joe asked.

"The straight and narrow I guess? I don't know. Either way, she said I would end up doing all these incredible things for God, that I would combine all my talents to spread the Gospel, and it was going to be big," I said.

"Interesting," Joe said.

I huffed a bit as I walked and talked. Joe and I walked everywhere in Boston, since we didn't have a car. We walked to and from school and work, to the train station, the grocery store, the movies.

Sometimes we took the fastest route, and sometimes we meandered, but we were always walking toward someplace, or away from another. "I think it's safe to say I've taken the meandering path," I said, laughing.

It had been six months since my embarrassing escapade in the bar, and I had recovered, and surprisingly my friendships had too. In fact, the incident seemed to solidify my bond with Allie, who told me not to worry about it, everyone has been there, which I appreciated, even though I suspected it wasn't true.

Besides feeling nauseated at the thought of fried chicken or Long Island iced tea, the experience left me with a peace I hadn't felt in years. Among friends, I could laugh at my sloppy antics, but inside I knew something important happened on the floor of that bar.

I thought about how long I'd spent searching for hope in the places I expected her—in church, in following rules, in being extraordinary for God—but not finding her until I ran from all that and wound up thrashing about in a pile of broken glass. Hope is a wily creature, isn't she? Always sneaking into places she's not supposed to be.

A chilly breeze tickled my face as I sat on a bench with my husband in our neighborhood park eating our warm breakfast. I wrapped my scarf around my neck a third time and rubbed my hands together. Our dog, a dachshund named Earl, chased a squirrel up a tree. We yelled at him to stop barking. A little girl around five years old walked by with her parents and squealed at the sight of a "wiener dog." Earl wiggled around, basking in the attention. Ten years ago, I thought I'd be immersed in whatever powerful thing I was called to do for God by now, perhaps running that nationwide creative arts Gospel revival, witnessing healing and salvation. Changing the world.

"I never thought I'd end up like this," I said, finishing off my croissant before it got cold. "I spent so long thinking I was chosen, or special, or something."

"And now you're un-chosen and un-special?" Joe asked, grinning.

"I guess so," I said.

I thought about that prophecy a lot during this time, and I decided that even if the direct route exists, of which I am skeptical, I am no longer interested in taking it. My obsession with this route ended when I discovered the beauty of being average, and by that I mean an ordinary screw-up like everyone else. An ordinary, beautiful screw-up.

Joe found a "community group" on Wednesday nights, and though I didn't like the sound of it, he'd been bugging me to join him for weeks, and I finally gave in.

"You'll like them, I promise," Joe said, as we walked to Jack and Valerie's apartment.

"I'll *like* church people?" I said.

"They aren't churchy. You'll see," he said. He led me to a brownstone and up five stories and opened the door to apartment 5B. I saw five or six people sitting on a rug drinking tea, and a tall, lanky Asian man jumped up to greet us.

"I'm Jack," he said. "You must be Carly. Joe has told us wonderful things about you. Come on in, can we get you something to drink? We were just talking about a book we're all reading about Henrietta Lacks, have you read it?"

"I actually haven't read it, but I've heard it's amazing," I said.

Joe glanced at me with an I-told-you-so look.

Valerie, Jack's wife, carried out a Meyer lemon cheesecake and everyone *oohed* and *aahed*.

"I don't know how you have time to bake in your last year of law school. You're just insane," someone said.

Valerie laughed. "Baking is how I pray. Some people find God in church. I don't. I find God when I'm in the kitchen and my apron is spattered with flour. Yeah, I know I'm weird," she said.

I looked at Joe, making a face that said "who are these people?" If Valerie meets God in the kitchen, I wondered if she would understand that I met God on the floor of a bar.

"So Carly and Joe, what is your story?" Jack asked, as we settled in for the lesson part of the evening. I didn't really know what to tell this room full of strangers.

"Well, we are students here in Boston. Kind of relearning everything, I guess. I used to be 'crazy for God.' And now I'm not. Now I don't even go to church," I said.

"I don't blame you," Valerie said. The rest of the group nodded like they understood. They didn't offer answers or open their Bibles in response.

Every Wednesday after this, Joe and I sat on the rug with our friends and Valerie's desserts, talking about God and books and culture. When they prayed out loud, I never joined, and they never asked me to.

Our last night together, before Joe and I were to move to California for new jobs, Jack and Valerie passed out flutes of champagne and made a toast to our next phase of life.

"We are thankful Joe and Carly crossed paths with us for this brief time," Jack prayed. "As they move on, may they roam and wander, and always find You in their midst."

Fourteen

I was perusing the art section in the Goodwill in Gilroy, California—our new home—one afternoon when I saw it: stacked between watercolor paintings of ducks wearing bonnets and faded photographs of the Statue of Liberty, the corner of a black-and-white poster I recognized immediately.

I rushed to pull it from the pile. There were the four Beatles, sideburns and unbuttoned coats and sad faces, the same print my brother framed for me when I was fourteen, the one I took down from my wall when I was sixteen, and the one I lost in the fire when I was seventeen. I ran my finger down the grooves of the broken frame, picking up dust under my nails. A sticker on the glass priced the print at six dollars. I stood in line to buy it, thinking about the person whose wall it came from, why it was taken down, how it ended up at the thrift store behind a bonneted duck.

Someone else might have seen it as just another Beatles poster, something to reframe and hang in the garage. But I loved it, broken frame and all. To me, it was a second chance.

—

The sign on the marquee listed a new pastor. I had been hearing rumors that Pastor Frank and Cindy retired a few years ago, but the sign made it real. I stepped out of my car, clutching a cup of black coffee from the local café. The potholes in the street had been patched up and new ones had formed. Moss grew in the upturned chunks of sidewalk leading to the church entrance. It was a Friday morning, and the gravel parking lot was empty. I walked up to the door, jostled the locked knob and stepped back, feeling like a trespasser in the place I'd once called home.

The building was now white with green trim, but the painted stucco was peeling in round, blotchy spots to reveal the stone gray color I remembered. I peered through the rotting windowsill, but couldn't see past the frosted glass. Several of the windows were broken, and cardboard had been taped to them from the inside.

I wondered where the legends about this church had originally come from. It had been a long time since I'd heard any Pine Canyon legends. I didn't hear much about Pine Canyon at all anymore. When I did visit, I spent time with family and then would head back to my adult life hours away.

I had thought coming here would bring back the memories of the control, the fear, the tears—but once here, that was not what I thought about at all. I remembered the games of Monkey in the Middle we played on Thursday nights while waiting for youth group to start. I remembered banging on the piano in the worst Christian band of all time and having fun doing it. I remembered my first time at Missionettes, how Candace treated me like I mattered. I remembered what it was like to close my eyes and feel like Jesus was so close I could smell him. I thought about how this is the last place I saw Kevin, that day I could smell the emptiness of his intestines in my car when I smashed his faith in God with a simple "no." Every few years I ask around to find out where he is. Nobody knows.

I thought about Kevin, sad and awkward in his see-though white T-shirts and cracked glasses, and how he kept showing up all those years because he was holding on to a dream from God, and how we would hate to admit it, but there was a piece of that in all of us. We all were like Kevin, believing in our dreams because our day-to-day lives were so empty.

I sat on the concrete ledge outside the front door where I used idle around with my friends for hours after church: laughing, singing, unaware that the magical sheen of youth would ever wear off. The legends about this place were both true and not true. I did come out, eventually. But a part of me still lives here. In the quiet, my eyes wandered to a blue Victorian cottage across the street. The front yard was a landscaped rock garden with camellias and climbing roses creeping up trellises and a stone wishing well. Two wicker rocking chairs were on the porch facing the garden. It's beautiful, I noticed for the first time. As I stared, a woman stepped outside the house and sat on her wicker chair with a mug of something steaming. She looked at me and smiled, and then leaned back and faced her garden. We each sipped our coffees, enjoying the silence of the morning.

The times I sat on this ledge before, I never once looked up. My whole world was the circle of people who lounged on that cracked concrete with me, and nothing outside that mattered.

I turned my eyes back to the church and in a brief, clear moment, I was struck with how small it was. I didn't feel any anger or resentment. I felt something else. Something sad, a dull ache, something close to pity—and not for me, but for the people who would worship there in two days, thinking they are on the cusp of seeing God do something huge. All these years I maintained this illusion of these big things happening here. That illusion was finally sinking, just like the roof on this old building. This place was so small, and the reason it still affected me was not because I was in its grips. It was in mine.

I loosened my fist and let go.

It was December 23, two days before my due date, but the doctor said no baby would be joining us for Christmas this year. The last time I weighed myself, I was pushing two hundred pounds, and every time I sat down, my sciatic nerve fired down my leg like an electric current. I was on my parents' couch in Pine Canyon, drinking chamomile tea and complaining to anyone who would listen. Inwardly though, I had never been more thrilled. I was having a baby.

I heard a knock on the door and waddled over.

"Merry Christmas, darling," Dahlia Platt cooed as I opened the door. She bent to kiss my belly. "And Merry Christmas to you, little darling."

Dahlia and I had sporadically kept in touch through the years. Dahlia never left Pine Canyon Assemblies of God. After finishing high school, she began to volunteer at youth group and eventually sang on the worship team for all twenty members who remained. Ten years ago, we were both belting Kelly Clarkson's *Breakaway* and dreaming about breaking away from our lives. I did, and she didn't. We have never talked about why I left or why she stayed.

She had two bottles in her hands—purple tinted lotion in her left and sparkling tangerine juice in her right.

"I've come to rub your feet," she said, and marched to the living room. "You lie here."

Mom and Dad came out and greeted Dahlia, whom they loved like family.

I lay on the couch, so grateful I felt like I might melt, and placed my feet on Dahlia's lap. My toes were pulsing. Dahlia squeezed a dollop of lotion and warmed it in her hands. The scent of lavender wafted in the air and calmed me instantly. She swirled her hands around my heel in firm healing rhythms.

"Oh Dahlia, this feels so good," I said. "It's like your hands carry the Spirit of God." It was a joke—and one that only a few people in my life would get—but it was also true.

We talked about possible names for the baby, and her recent trip to Hawaii. She said she would be taking a team of teens to Mexico in the summer, and she was excited about the ways God will move there.

"God is just doing some incredible stuff with the youth at church," she said, circling her thumbs around my anklebone. "Everyone is on fire."

"Mmm-hmm," I said. I was gliding out of consciousness at her touch. Her language was so familiar, yet so foreign at the same time. It was a language I no longer spoke, but I noticed it didn't incite rage anymore either. My heart was at peace. I was about to have a baby. My old friend was with me. She was rubbing my feet. She was right: God was doing incredible stuff.

A month later, I was still getting the hang of breastfeeding my newborn girl, Georgie, when Dahlia came to visit for a couple days. Stuck inside, and dressed in yoga pants, we ate frozen pizza and talked as Georgie slept on me, fed on me, and spat up on me. We laughed about all the nights we danced in the Starbucks parking lot, how alive we'd felt on a park swing. Our voices lowered when we reflected on the many times we got in trouble together.

"Well, can you blame us? We used to get lectured if we used the word *boob*," I said, unbuttoning my blouse to try to latch my squirmy infant for feeding time.

"They were always watching," she said. "We were so afraid of them."

"It was all pretty messed up," I said. "Kind of abusive, really."

Dahlia paused, and stared at the rug. I could tell she was hurt.

"They weren't perfect, but their hearts were good. I'm still so thankful for their influence in my life," she said.

I gave a half-nod but didn't respond. I didn't know how to. I didn't need to explain to Dahlia how it was. She had been there for all of it, even the night in the upper room, yet she saw it differently. At one point, I had asked her about Leah and her face went blank. She said they don't talk much anymore. I didn't press it. I decided to reach out to Leah for myself.

I stared at Leah's Facebook profile picture, shocked. She was smiling in a flowing, strapless white dress with a long train in a meadow at dusk. She looked the same as I remembered, only with more stylish hair. Another woman, dressed in a vest and bow tie, kissed her cheek and held a bouquet of lilies to their faces. After a moment of disbelief, I began piecing things together.

Alongside everything else that was happening around us, all the normal turmoil of being a fundamentalist teenager, Leah had been in the closet the whole time. All this time, when I thought of Leah, I pictured her at Pine Canyon Assemblies of God—and I understood the self-centered nature of that assumption, that I'd spent ten years growing and changing but I'd kept Leah static, stunting her as the same person she was at sixteen. Just as I'd spent the last decade growing and changing and stringing those small choices together to make something new, Leah had done the same thing. Leah had spent these years making the choices it took to become the blushing bride in this photo. Her choices were no doubt harder.

I hovered my cursor over the "Request Friend" button,

gathering the nerve to click it. We never talked about the animosity between us all these years. I still didn't know what role she'd played that night in the upper room, if she had complained to Jessa about me and instigated the whole thing. If I added her, would she even accept?

I wasn't sure, but I knew I had to try. I sent a message along with my friend request, since I thought she might not have recognized me with my married name.

"Hey, Leah," I wrote. Be friendly, but neutral, I thought as I typed. "I just wanted to message you because I'm remembering some of the things we've been through together, and you've been on my mind. Hope you are well."

Within seconds, she accepted my friend request and a few minutes later, my screen flashed with a message from her.

"Hi, Carly! I'm so happy you wrote me. I agree. It took me a long time of processing to realize what craziness we were put through. I have grown and changed so much since then, and it is nice to finally be really, truly happy. Thank you for messaging me. It is so good to hear from you."

We sent messages back and forth for a few days, and when she announced a few months later that she and her wife were pregnant with twins, I teared up. There was a picture of her on Facebook, beaming and holding her big belly out for the camera. She did look happy.

I hobbled through the early days of motherhood, perpetually tired and glazed-eyed. One day, Georgie was playing on our living room rug with the blocks she received for her first birthday. I sat on the couch with a second cup of coffee. She carefully piled one block over another, until her tower stood taller than her. The wobbly structure would fall soon, and I clenched myself for the toddler meltdown when it did.

But then the strangest thing happened. The blocks crashed around Georgie, and she didn't cry. She smiled big and clapped her chubby hands and began to re-stack them one by one.

This happened over and over. Build, fall, rebuild. I sat there, amazed. I was amazed by my daughter's tenacity and playfulness, in the way all smitten new parents are, but I was amazed by something else too, something I couldn't name.

"Thank you," I whispered, and caught myself off guard. Was that a prayer? It couldn't be—there were no mashed knees on the carpet, no claiming victory. But there was something so familiar about it, something so natural, and I knew I was talking to God.

Crash. Georgie squealed at the rubble around her and began building again. *This is revival*, I thought. Building from collapsed pieces, again and again. I thought back to the days I yearned for revival, those summer nights on park swings. Revival was always about to happen, and I believed I could bring it by fasting and staying on my knees and reciting the right scriptures. When it happened, it would be big.

I never did see that that kind of revival. Instead, it crept up on me when I wasn't looking. I saw it in an old poster at the thrift store, in the embrace of an old friend. I felt it coming over me, block by block, a slow and steady process of awakening.

There had to be a church that worshipped the God I found on floors, with broken glass or toy blocks surrounding me. I set out to find it.

We tried the Cool Church across town, the one full of young, thin people with crucifix tattoos and skinny jeans. Several weeks in a row we showed up and made painful small talk with people, grasping to get into their community. But we were outsiders, unable to penetrate their inner sanctum of fellowship. After a couple of weeks, I started to notice that underneath the hipster veneer at this church, they were selling the same stuff I had run from.

"I'm not the kind of guy who's going to tell you what you want to hear," the pastor often said from the pulpit. "Because I'm not going to water down the Truth of the Gospel!"

But I was beginning to wonder if the *Truth of the Gospel* was something different than he preached. When I read the Gospel, I saw Jesus saying, "Come to me, all who are weary." I saw him blessing the poor and the weak and bringing life to the lifeless, respite for the tired. I saw him challenging authorities and questioning the righteous, and hanging out with the screw-ups. I thought for the first time, maybe faith is about accepting a downpour of hope for dry souls. I wanted to be around other people in the downpour.

We stopped trying at the Cool Church. Months later, we tried a Bible Study at a Community Church up the road from us, hoping to find something like Jack and Valerie's group.

The leader, a freckled kid studying the Bible at an online seminary, seemed to be anxious to show off his expository chops. He led a study of a passage in Hosea, in which he looked for specific answers from the group to corral the discussion in the direction he planned.

"What do you think God is talking about in that passage?" he asked the group.

"Forgiveness?" said one guy.

"Hmm, maybe forgiveness, but also perseverance, which leads me to my next point."

We sat in fold-up chairs in the backyard, our butts vaguely sore from the hard plastic that cocooned them. At one point, the leader's cat sauntered up to our circle. Joe leaned over to pet the fat thing as the freckled leader continued his lecture.

"You don't have to pet the cat if you don't want to," the leader said.

"Oh, I want to," Joe said. I recognized the spark in his eyes. He picked up the cat and scratched its ears and cooed little terms of endearment. The cat meowed in pleasure.

"Really, you don't have to do that," the leader said, more uncomfortable.

"Please, don't you worry about me," Joe said, grinning.

The leader went back to his exposition of Hosea as Joe fussed over the cat on his lap. The leader's face was getting red, and his shoulders were stiff. Every few minutes he'd dart another look at Joe.

"Really, the devil comes in all forms to distract us," he said, motioning to the cat. I giggled nervously. Joe met eyes with the leader while he continued to pet the cat in deliberate long strokes.

When his sermon was finished, I singled out the leader's wife, who wore a kind smile. She had sat close to her husband and scratched his back the entire time.

"And what do you do?" I asked.

"I'm in my second year at San Jose State," she said.

"What are you studying?"

"Early childhood education," she said. "I love it so far. It's the best."

The leader, fidgeting, piped in.

"It's so she can be a good mom," he said.

"That's not why I chose my major," the wife said quietly and shook her head.

"It is if I say so!" he said, laughing, and patted his young wife on the knee. The conversation was over. Joe and I exchanged a look and got up to leave. It was getting late.

We tried nearly every church in our end of the county, big

churches and small churches and young churches and old churches. We had given up on finding what we were searching for. We began to take long walks on Sunday mornings instead, and found great solace in this family tradition.

We were taking a long walk on a winter Sunday morning, pushing Georgie in a stroller through neighborhoods of small homes with dogs barking in the yard, colorful Victorians and ivy-covered brick fences, and through parks with children playing soccer and men on bicycles selling horchata and sliced fruit. After trekking several miles, we agreed to end our stroll at the local donut shop. On our way, we passed a church with stained glass windows and a copper bell mounted in a tower. We could hear choral music coming from inside.

I stopped and listened. The doors were open.

"Mind if we get donuts later?" I said. "I'd like to poke our heads in."

Joe looked a little confused—we had never been to an Episcopal church together, let alone any church for months—but he shrugged and followed me.

A few dozen people were standing in front of sturdy oak pews, reading out loud from the Psalms. The room smelled of hot wax, a lot like the Orthodox Church in Romania. We pushed the stroller to one of the pews in the back and sat. We mumbled along with the recitations and quietly sang along to the songs. Georgie was shrieking and flapping her hands.

I didn't know why I was there, yet I did.

We knelt at our pew after we looked around and noticed everyone else was kneeling. I closed my eyes for a moment and was taken back to those Sundays visiting my grandmother's Episcopal church as a little girl. I could see her wrinkled face glowing, her hands raised and eyes closed as she sang the Doxology. I could recall how woozy I felt after eating my first communion wafer dipped in real wine, how the room spun as I stepped from the altar to the prayer receiving line, where my grandmother hugged me, so proud and strong. I could feel people putting their hands on my shoulders and hear them saying "Peace be with you."

"You must be Ann's granddaughter."

"Peace be with you."

"Ann is the jewel of our crown—and to think, you are a jewel in hers."

"Peace be with you."

Grandma had died the first winter I spent in Boston. When she left, she took with her another little piece of my faith. So much of my relationship with God in my teen years had been rooted in the abstract, the future, the spiritual realm. Grandma was my tangible counterpoint to all of that. She was grace adorned with pink lipstick from Thrifty's. Her body wasn't next to me in those pews that day, but I was taken back to the feeling of belonging I felt when I was near her. Of God's presence. Of peace.

My thoughts were brought back to reality by a squealing Georgie running up and down our pew. She threw a Cheerio on the carpet and looked at me with a mischievous glint in her eyes. Embarrassed for the scene my latecomer family was creating, I picked her up and took her out of the sanctuary, leaving Joe alone in our pew.

I was wearily watching Georgie walk in circles in the church courtyard when a woman tapped me on the shoulder and looked me in the eye. "What are you doing out here?" she said. "We believe the most beautiful worship of all is the sound of a baby's cry." Taken aback, I carried my daughter inside, and she fussed and laughed and clapped throughout the rest of the service. We went forward as a family for communion, Georgie squirming in my arms. The white-robed priest gently touched her forehead.

"God the Father, God the Son, and God the Holy Spirit bless and keep you all the days of your life," he said. The *Alleluias* went up around us, and each one filled me with a tiny bit of something that felt a tiny bit like faith.

I didn't wash up at the Episcopal Church for theology, although I've since found a healing balm in the Book of Common Prayer. I came because their doors were open one day, and they welcomed my mangy family, with our crushed Cheerios and bad attitudes.

Fifteen

I t's my first weekend away since Georgie was born and I'm spending it in Seattle with Eleanor. This is a special reunion for us, and a retreat from our daily lives. Our Yelp searches have led us to a midtown lounge far fancier than we would have picked ourselves, but we are happy to be here nonetheless. We talk in our cushioned booth in the low-lit lounge, enjoying the ease of a friendship in its second decade.

The bartender, a young man dressed in a newsboy hat and tweed vest overhears us.

"Did I hear you say this is a special occasion?" he asks, grinning. He has a spark in his eyes and he gets to work behind the counter. A few minutes later, he brings two drinks to our table served in hollowed-out passion fruit.

"It's a green tea infused sparkler with crushed blueberries," he says, proud. "On the house." We ogle his creation and Eleanor takes a photo for Instagram.

Eleanor and I have spent the majority of the weekend remembering, venting, and making sense of our crazy God days. While she still believes, Eleanor fell away from the burning faith of her youth a while back, much as I did, although neither of us talked much about it during the painful process of leaving. Now we look back together. And still we sometimes find ourselves short for words.

Joe texts me a picture of Georgie from earlier that day: she's wearing a teal polka dot shirt and orange striped shorts, a thick layer of mud smeared on her puffy cheeks. I pass the photo to Eleanor, who coos. Eleanor is now a nurse in a trauma center emergency room, where she confronts death, disease, addictions, and mental disorders on a daily basis.

"It's not like I don't want to *change the world* anymore. I do," she says. "It just looks different than it used to."

"I get that."

"I want to nurse people back to health and be friends with the people we used to turn up our noses at," she says.

"You mean you don't want to *shake the nations* anymore?" I say, winking.

"No. I'm far too backslidden for that," she says.

We laugh. We've embraced the backslidden label now, in a tongue-and-cheek way. We sip our passion fruit drinks slowly, not to get drunk, but to relax into the evening as adults.

"I have something for you," Eleanor says. She reaches into her purse and hands me a folded piece of lined notebook paper.

"To my rad friend. Do not open until you get home," it reads on the front. My heart freezes, because I know what I'm holding. It's a letter I wrote Eleanor on the last day of our mission trip to Romania so long ago.

"I can't read this. I can't," I say.

"Then I'll read it to you," she says, reaching for the note.

"No!" I shout, pulling it away from her. "I'm going to throw it away."

But even as I say this, I'm unfolding the paper, knowing I was going to read it all along.

Dear Ellie, God's got an incredible plan for you, and I'll be praying for you. Let's take our mission field home and shake up our worlds with our faith! I pray we can stay strong and rock for Jesus! In my loopy fifteen-year-old handwriting.

An involuntary groan rises from my throat.

"This doesn't sound like me. Seriously, who even wrote this?" I say.

Let's set our friends on fire! The note continues.

"I sound like an arsonist," I say, slapping my forehead.

Keep being a REBEL because rebels rock! I read, remembering our last night in Romania, how we were rebels for sleeping on the floor.

I finish the letter, take a sip from my drink, fold the letter back up, and take a deep breath.

"So we were a little crazy. But we had caught this passion for God, and we thought our God needed us to spread that passion to the ends of the earth," I say. "We were just kids trying to do that."

"We were just kids. And it was sincere," she says.

"When did it start?" I ask. "The backsliding. When did it begin?"

Eleanor pauses and swirls her passion fruit around in her fist.

"Honestly, I don't know."

"But try and think about it."

For me, I think it began when I left Pine Canyon Assemblies of God after the night of the Reckoning. Or it could have began the day I drove to church, turned off the car, and sat in silence for five minutes with my hand on the gear shifter before restarting the car, shifting to reverse and driving away. Or maybe it was before that. Maybe it began the night I picked at the green paint on my wrists in that El Paso hotel, as Cindy expressed concern that my heart was growing cold for Jesus.

But it could have been before all that for all I know.

It could have been my date with Marco, or my doubts about the Holy Spirit, even as I spoke in tongues at the altar. It could have been the night when, in the solitude of my bedroom, I chose to listen to the Beatles instead of a worship CD after I promised God I would give up secular music.

Who knows?

"I think it must have started a long time ago," Eleanor says.

"They were always saying it all begins with one tiny sin."

"Maybe they were right."

"Maybe they were," I say. "But they never told us that when we do slide to the bottom, we learn about grace."

"And we figure out we're going to be okay."

I finish off my drink, place the empty passion fruit on our candlelit table, and watch it roll sideways. I lean back in my chair, grateful for whatever tiny sin led me here.

Months later, visiting my parents, Mom, Dad, Joe, and I are sitting in plastic lawn chairs in their backyard watching Georgie play with water balloons in her splash pool. The air is warm but tempered by a breeze crawling up the canyon.

Mom gasps when she checks the date on her smartphone. "It's today."

I already knew, but hadn't mentioned it. It's the ten-year anniversary of the fire.

"Can you imagine?" she says. "Ten years."

"Amazing what ten years can do."

Trees speckle the property again. Not as large or thick as they used to be, of course, as nature takes decades on decades to replenish itself. A bulbous sycamore tree, which burnt to the ground ten years ago to the day, has grown back. When the first sign of life sprouted from the tree's blackened base eight years ago or so, we were shocked.

Now the sycamore's knuckled branches stretch over the deck at my parents' home, providing shade for summer barbecues, and proving its resilience.

In the mornings, fog can be seen rising from the canyon's grooves, and in the evenings, the sun disappears under shades of pink and orange clouds. It will never look the same as it did before, but it was beautiful then and beautiful now. I think about the years I worried God started the fire to punish us, and I laugh. Who knows why the fire ravaged the canyon? A propane spark started it, sure, but there's no way to know what leads to what, or why, or where I would be right now if the fire hadn't happened, or if I'd never gone to that Christian camp so long ago, or if Danny didn't have a secret girlfriend, or if I hadn't been forced away from the faith I'd clung to so tightly. What matters is that I'm here. I've moved eight times in the past ten years, and have recently bought a house in Gilroy, a community I love and plan to grow roots in. But in many ways, this piece of land will always be home.

A bee buzzes around me, and I don't swat it away. I think of the days I thought I was a Voice to this Desert. This canyon I call home is not a Desert, not in any literal or metaphorical or spiritual sense. Our lakes and rivers are fresh and deep, just like our people. We may not be the type to sit in a church pew on Sundays, but our hearts are lush with the image of God.

Georgie points to her diaper and shouts "off!" in that clipped, deliberate way toddlers talk. I lean over and peel off the heavy diaper from her skin. She jiggles her bottom and basks in her nakedness.

She will never know the ways the fire permanently changed this landscape. But I will try to tell her.

My fire for God changed me, and while I never want to go back, I can see hope is leading the way to something good. It has led me to the slow growth of faith, of small shoots of life pushing up from dead stumps, of expansive views of hope I may have never seen otherwise.

And I know it's not over, not in the least. New life will emerge as old life ebbs away, and droughts and storms will keep coming and changing the earth. This is the beauty of it all. I will keep questioning and thanking and running and falling and searching and rebuilding, because this is the process of being alive. Revival is here, in this land and inside me, and has been here all along, taking decay and turning it and churning it to create life.

Georgie finds a stick lying in the grass and begins whipping it into the water, splashing my knees with little cool drops.

"I wonder what the next ten years will bring," I say, but as soon as the words come out, I realize I'm not really wondering at all. I am immersed in the moment, in the drops of water on my leg, my daughter's dimpled thighs, the bee buzzing around my hair, and the canyon behind me.

ACKNOWLEDGMENTS

This book is a labor of love and I am in awe at the number of people who helped bring it to life.

Thank you to Brooke Warner and the team at She Writes Press for your passion, not only for my story, but for the work you do to honor women's voices in literature.

Every author needs an Andy Meisenheimer. Thank you for all the work you did on this manuscript and for fighting for it through all its incarnations. And for the life-changing advice you gave me in 2016 when I felt barred by the gatekeepers of Christian publishing. You told me to run the other way to save my book, and my soul. *Suffer for your art. It's the only way.* You were right.

Emily Maynard, who critiqued the earliest versions of this book years ago, many thanks. You helped me find that voice of the adolescent girl who carries this story. Your fingerprints are all over these pages.

Emily Camera, Laura Sierra, and Julie McQuieter, my dear friends whose stories cross with my own. Thank you for all the input along the way, for jogging my memory of what those Pentecostal services were like, and for helping me laugh throughout the writing process.

Thanks to every single soul I've brushed paths with who encouraged me to keep going, including the barista at the Gilroy Barnes & Noble who poured me free coffee as I clunked out the first draft. To my in-laws, Pat and Linda Gelsinger, I appreciate all your support for my writing through the years, from the clipping of my first newspaper story to reading my thoughts on faith, which you disagree with in the classiest way possible.

Thank you to my parents for instilling me with dreams, creativity, and fresh air, which are the building blocks for any writing career. You gave me everything.

I am indebted to my writer friends who critiqued and gave feedback in big and small ways: Meghan Foley, Lauren Shields, Andi Joseph, Vince Favilla, Stephen Carter, Kelsey Munger, Cindy Brandt, and Ed Cyzewski, and to Liz Boltz-Ranfeld who took me in, in more than one way. I also am in a place of huge gratitude to the authors who generously encouraged me early on with kind words: Elizabeth Esther, Reba Riley, Maggie Rowe, Jennifer Knapp, and David Gushee.

I am grateful for every person in this story who led me to where I am today. Beth Kephart once said that memoir isn't fair because it captures the growth and change of the author while keeping other people frozen in time. I have found that to be true. There are no villains or heroes in this story—just people muddling through.

To my students at Gavilan Community College: I've learned more about writing from you than I have anywhere else. Thank you for sharing your incredible stories with me.

Georgiana and Abigail, not only did you put up with the hundreds of hours I spent writing, but you kept me grounded in the here and now when I needed to be.

And to JPG, where do I begin? Thanks for doing those countless loads of laundry as I birthed this book. You are my reason.

DISCUSSION QUESTIONS

1. Why do you think Carly joined the church? What did the church offer her at the time?

2. Do you think her experience with speaking in tongues was real? Why or why not?

3. In Chapter Five, Jessa tells Carly she is special and marked for God. In what ways do you think this changed Carly's faith?

4. Why do you think Carly's faith circles used fire as a spiritual metaphor?

5. What was it about Danny that drew Carly in? Have you ever been drawn to someone in a similar way?

6. Carly changed herself to be accepted. Have you ever conformed for a similar reason? What were the consequences?

7. What did you think of the role Carly's parents played in her journey in and out of the church?

8. Some of Carly's actions are appalling, such as blowing out the candles in the Orthodox Church, and faking a prophecy in

front of her whole school. As a reader, could you understand her choices, or did you find her unsympathetic? Why or why not?

9. Toward the end of the book, Carly talks a lot about "the fog." It seems clear to readers that she was suffering from clinical depression. Why didn't she seek professional help?

10. Why do you think Kevin held on to the dream of marrying Carly for so long, despite her never showing interest? Why did Carly hold on to Danny?

11. The book begins with what readers may at first think was Carly's rock bottom. What do you think was her actual rock bottom?

12. Carly describes Pentecostalism as "the cousin who shows up for Thanksgiving in a colorful wrap dress while everyone else is in Dockers and Polo shirts." But later, she finds evangelicalism to be as damaging as the crazy Pentecostals they made fun of. Do you agree with her conclusion?

13. Cults can be found anywhere, not just in religious circles. Have you experienced any of the similar patterns of manipulation, control, and leadership adulation in other communities, such as the workplace, school, sports teams, clubs, etc.?

About the Author

Carly Gelsinger lives in California with her husband and two daughters. She holds a master's in journalism and runs a small business helping people write their stories. This is her first book.

SELECTED TITLES FROM SHE WRITES PRESS

She Writes Press is an independent publishing company founded to serve women writers everywhere. Visit us at www.shewritespress.com.

Manifesting Me: A Story of Rebellion and Redemption
by Leah E. Reinhart. $16.95, 978-1-63152-383-0
When Leah Reinhart was six years old, her family joined a cult in Oakland, California—and she spent much of her life afterward trying to break free of the damaging patterns she was taught there.

Uncovered: How I Left Hassidic Life and Finally Came Home
by Leah Lax. $16.95, 978-1-63152-995-5
Drawn in their offers of refuge from her troubled family and promises of eternal love, Leah Lax becomes a Hassidic Jew—but ultimately, as a forty-something woman, comes to reject everything she has lived for three decades in order to be who she truly is.

The Burn Zone: A Memoir by Renee Linnell
$16.95, 978-1-63152-487-5
By the age of fifteen, Renee had lost almost everyone she loved; seeking answers, she set out on a quest for spiritual enlightenment and understanding—only to find herself entrenched in a Buddhist cult.

Fourteen: A Daughter's Memoir of Adventure, Sailing, and Survival
by Leslie Johansen Nack. $16.95, 978-1-63152-941-2
A coming-of-age adventure story about a young girl who comes into her own power, fights back against abuse, becomes an accomplished sailor, and falls in love with the ocean and the natural world.

Lost in the Reflecting Pool: A Memoir by Diane Pomerantz
$16.95, 978-1-63152-268-0
A psychological story about Diane, a highly trained child psychologist, who falls in love with Charles, a brilliant and charming psychiatrist—ignoring all the red flags that will later come back to haunt her.

The S Word by Paolina Milana
$16.95, 978-1-63152-927-6
An insider's account of growing up with a schizophrenic mother, and the disastrous toll the illness—and her Sicilian Catholic family's code of secrecy—takes upon her young life.